God Is Not a Boy's Name

GOD
Is Not a Boy's Name

Becoming Woman, Becoming Priest

To dear Honor —
Carry on with
grit and grace —
with deep affection,
Lyn
June, 2017

The Rev. Lyn G. Brakeman

 CASCADE *Books* · Eugene, Oregon

GOD IS NOT A BOY'S NAME
Becoming Woman, Becoming Priest

Cascade Books
An Imprint of Wipf and Stock Publishers
199 W. 8th Ave., Suite 3
Eugene, OR 97401

www.wipfandstock.com

ISBN 13: 978-1-4982-2627-1

Cataloging-in-Publication data:

Brakeman, Lyn G.

God is not a boy's name : becoming woman, becoming priest / Lyn G. Brakeman.

xii + 180 p.; 23 cm.

ISBN 13: 978-1-4982-2627-1

1. Brakeman, Lyn. 2. Episcopal Church Clergy Biography 3. Episcopalians Biography

BX5995.B69 2016

Manufactured in the USA.

For Mom, whose tenacity brought me into life and gave me God.
For Dad, who showed me the point of good religion and soul-seriousness.
For both parents, who loved me imperfectly with perfectly good intentions
and helped me become a priest.

For my sister Laurie, who stuck by me through thick and thin.

For my children, natural and acquired through love, without whose
graciousness my life and vocation would not have thrived.

For Dick, my husband most gracious, a natural theatric,who read most of
this story aloud to me just to let me know how it sounded.

For all friends and writing buddies, casual and professional, who have ever
touched my life with grace. You all know who you are, and god knows God
knows who you are.

And for God, whose three-personed name is unflinchingly hallowed and
genderless.

Table of Contents

TABLE OF CONTENTS

Introduction

In the 1940s, when I was a child, God was named He, Him, His, Himself. Today God is still named He, Him, His, Himself. I knew from the beginning, however, and came to know more deeply as time went on, that God was not male—despite evidence to the contrary in churches, and even in common parlance. My odd spiritual awareness came to me through the experience of a little girl under a big dining table—and a T-shirt.

When I was three and two-thirds exactly, I had my first spiritual adventure. I remember my age, because it was before my sister was born, and I was still an only child—adored and adorable. My mother thought I was a miracle and told me I was a gift from God. Miracle status made me squirm, but the God idea had promise. It provided courage and curiosity enough for me to one evening lose patience with my parents' nightly cocktail hour and huff off on my own to conquer the world, or at least to find a new one. Well supplied with Ritz crackers from the cocktail tray, I crawled under our large dining room table with cross beams and a cloth to the floor. Under that table, three worlds of wonder opened up to me simultaneously: the world of words, the world of being a girl, and the world of God.

Under my table I discovered a God who listened to my every word with no judgment, a God who let me know I mattered, no matter what. Was this the God who had given me to my mother as a gift? In a favorite book I saw God sitting in a garden listening to all the sounds on earth, even weeny sounds like mine. I bonded to this intimate, listening image, and held it dear. Although this God had a long white beard and was clearly male, it didn't matter to me—until five years later when an old man with a long white beard sexually molested me in a theater. He might as well have been God. I lost my agency, my authority, and my connection to my body. I nearly lost sight of God. Nearly.

I went on to do all the usual things for a woman of my class and privilege—college, marriage, children, chocolate chip cookies. It was not until the 1970s that I first saw the bright blue T-shirt bearing the slogan, "God Is Not a Boy's Name," written in pretty white script—womanly. It was one of the campaign slogans coined by women who were pushing the patriarchal Episcopal Church to ordain them priests. There on that shirt, for the very first time, I saw the outer sign of the inner conviction I'd had as a little girl: God is not male, even though He is called He.

I bought the shirt, tried it on once, puffed up my chest, and looked in the mirror. Then I placed it into my dresser drawer for safekeeping. From its hiding place, the shirt drove me on, and into, a long, passionate fight with the Episcopal Church to be ordained a priest. I was an institutional naif, a budding feminist, mother of four children, and suburbanly bored housewife on fire for my vision. I was also in a whirlwind of midlife personal chaos.

The Episcopal Church was in its own whirlwind. There were changes in all the staples of its political and liturgical life: new Book of Common Prayer, new catechism, and new Hymnal—not to mention a change in clergy gender. In 1976 the National Church finally voted that women could be priests. Immeasurable spiritual zeal, combined with midlife hormones, made me irresistible, I thought. The church disagreed—more than once. I kept on trying—more than once.

Memory, and writing, and my children's unfolding lives gave me hope while I binged on the exhilarating, joyfully insane, delicious power of freedom. I'd heard that freedom was a divine gift; I didn't know it was also dangerous and devilishly hard to navigate, worse than a whirlwind. Still, I was a woman fully alive—seeking God, meeting Jesus, rediscovering the power of my personal sexuality, exploring the politics of gender equality, drinking too much, grieving painful losses, and nearly sinking. Nearly.

The Eucharist, a meal that was punctual and regular and nurturing, gave me religious stability. It was a sacrament that fed me anyway, and through which I recognized an embodiment of the intimacy I had once known and now craved. The Eucharist is served from an altar. It replicated the Ritz cracker meal I'd invented under the table.

Ordination made me a priest, a vocation that continued to evolve as I continued to become a fully realized human being. These two maturation processes intertwined and still do. The more I presided at Eucharist, the more I noticed that women and girls continued to get short shrift in society and church—injustice in my world *and* God's. I retrieved the old T-shirt and wore it like a vestment as I kept lobbying for my conviction that God is not male, and further, that Christianity needs a just and loving language for humanity *and* divinity. It is idolatry to worship an all-male deity we know has no gender. I had to tell the whole story.

God Is Not a Boy's Name is written in gratitude: for the meeting of God and a little girl under a table, for the quirky wisdom of a T-shirt, for the upcoming fortieth anniversary of the historic 1976 vote to ordain women priests in the Episcopal Church, and for the fact that, so far, no one has ever been brash enough to include God as a choice in one of those books that lists name choices for children.

CHAPTER 1 Under the Table

I was born through tears, none of them mine and all of them cried before I emerged to contribute my own. My mother had suffered three miscarriages, wept often on her doctor's shoulder, and stormed heaven with her prayers. My first life achievement was hanging in there for nine months. I've been tenacious ever since.

It was high summer in 1938 when I whooshed into life, breaking my mother's waters and interrupting my parents' winning bridge game six weeks before a hurricane blasted the Northeast. Nineteen-thirty-eight was a teetery year between wars, but full of hope for prosperity and a brand-new line of Buicks, the car of choice for our family. It was Sunday, a day the church called holy and my mother called my personality, according to the rhyme: "The child that is born on the Sabbath day is blithe and bonnie and good and gay." Sunday or no Sunday, her choice for my theme song never fit my personality—silent, somber, serious, and shy. Mom was the one full of gaiety and energy. From an early age I wished she would alight.

Dad gave me my name, Lynda with a "y" to call me Lyn or Lynnie, as well as his handsome features, thick dark hair, and introversion. He worked on Madison Avenue advertising soups, and my mother stayed home and advertised me. I was, she said, "my father's child." Such a dedication might have set me to wondering whether I was her child, but I didn't because of her studious determination to remake me in her image, putting little bows in my unruly hair and daily dressing me in frilly pinafores. The red party shoes were acceptable, but honestly, the only good thing about pinafores was their "wings." I wanted some hair-rumpling hugs that mussed me up but I don't remember many. Still: I got something more, something that would intrigue me for the rest of my life.

"You are a miracle and a gift from God, Lynnie," my mother told me more than once.

1

"What's a miracle?" I asked.

"Something God does for us that we can't do for ourselves," she said. "I wanted a baby and I kept losing them. Miscarriage, it's called. And then you came."

"But didn't I come from a hospital?" I asked.

"Of course, LeRoy Sanitarium, a maternity hospital in downtown Manhattan," she said.

I would have kept up my questioning, but my mother had that "enough" look and turned aside. So I pondered my near-divinity on my own. Miracle status was problematic, in part because it earned me excesses of maternal praise and made me feel almost breakable, and in part because my younger sister Laurie never made it to miracle status, even though Mom had two miscarriages before her birth. I was just plain too miraculous for comfort. Being a gift from God, however, had promise. Who was God? What kind of gift was I? Where was God? I wanted to meet God.

I'd seen God in a book called *The Little Book About God* published just four years before I was born. It became my favorite book, so favorite my mother got sick of it. I still have it, crayon marks and all. God was an old man with a long white beard perched on a cloud and creating wonders on earth far below. In the city where we lived everything reached up, like an alleluia hymn, so on our daily playground walks I held tightly to the carriage and trained my gaze skyward searching for God. I never saw God up there though, so maybe my book's sky-God wasn't all there was to God.

Nightly, Mom and I prepared for Daddy's homecoming. I shed the pinafore and hair bows. We bathed. Mom dressed me in a not-too-frilly nightgown, and herself in a lavender negligée and mules with open toes. She sat at her dressing table, prettying herself with bright red lipstick, rouge on her cheeks, and perfume behind her ears. I got a daub on my wrist. A cigarette hung out of one side of Mom's mouth, causing her eye to squint as she brushed my hair to a sheen and said out of the other side of her mouth, "Isn't this fun, darling?"

I nodded, held my nose, and requested some lipstick, which Mom spread on lightly with her fingertip.

"It's just for girls," she said. "The bewitching hour because we love Daddy." My mother taught me vanity and an awareness that appearances could help me feel good-all-over feminine.

I begged for a book. "Just one, a short one, please, please, Mommy." She read *The Children's Hour* by Henry Wadsworth Longfellow. I held my breath.

> Between the dark and the daylight,
> When the night is beginning to lower,
> Comes a pause in the day's occupations,
> That is known as the Children's Hour.

I think my mother and I both longed for the children's hour. It evoked a hope that hung unspoken in the air between us: *This night will be different.* But every night the Children's Hour turned into the Cocktail Hour. Daddy would come in the door and we'd both run to meet him. He tossed his newspaper aside and picked me up for a kiss. His cheek was grizzly and tickled mine. He smelled like tobacco. "Smell my perfume, Daddy." I held my wrist to his nose as he carried me to the bedroom where he changed into his velvet-lapeled smoking jacket. Then we all went into the living room. An hors d'oeuvres tray sat on the table in front of the blue-and-white sofa. Daddy sat in his Daddy chair, which had wings like my pinafores did. I sat in my small rocker. The stage was set for my mother's entrance. She appeared on cue with the drinks on a tray, her large Coke and Daddy's large cocktail shaker and his favorite glass—shaped like a triangle with a long slender stem and three enormous green cross-eyed olives nestled in its bottom. It was one of the few times my mother's butterfly soul alighted. She riveted her attention on Daddy, who twirled the omnipotent glass and took sips. That glass sucked up all the attention I wanted for myself. We could've been in church for all the awe this ritual commanded.

"Can I have a sip, Daddy?" I asked, breaking the spell.

"Not for little girls," he said.

"Mommy?" I said, and got a sip from her glass. I wondered if olive-filled glasses were for men only.

I rocked at breakneck speed and hummed little tunes, but no one noticed. Fed up at last, I gave up. I snatched Ritz crackers from the cocktail tray and huffed off, with the stomp of three-year-old feet. It sometimes seemed to me that my feet knew where they were going before I did. That was certainly the case as I exited the cocktail hour, hearing my father, by now turned martini-nasty, say as I left, "She only wants all those crackers for herself."

I found a place and invented a ritual of my own under the dining room table, which had cross beams to connect its four fat legs and a cloth to the floor. At first I felt lonely and lost, so I removed my slippers and placed them outside the tablecloth so my parents would know where I was; then I lined the Ritz crackers up on a beam and sat cross-legged on the worn maroon rug. To make company I began to chat to my three imaginary friends when a fourth friend joined us—very silent, extremely invisible. I had longed to be noticed, yet suddenly discovered a mysterious freedom in going unnoticed. That's when I knew I mattered and decided that this fourth friend must be the God I longed to meet. With delight I unburdened my soul. God listened to me with an attentiveness neither of my parents, distracted at this hour by an ugly glass, nor my distractible imaginary friends could give. After our conversation I served a one-course meal under the table. I ate one Ritz cracker and left four on the beam, partly to prove something to my father and partly because it was plain polite.

At bedtime, my mother called for kisses and took me to bed. In the morning the crackers were still there, just as I'd left them.

Not for some time did I realize that I would not have picked out the little God book for myself. It had no splashy illustrations and I couldn't read. My mother picked it out for me. How did she know I would love it, or did she love it for me? Another portrait of God in the book was earthy and true to my experience:

> When God was sitting in His garden very quietly, He began to hear a sound coming up from His Earth and the sound was like the buzzing of a great far-away bee. And God became very interested. And He began to listen, and separate it, one sound from another, and to find the place that each came from. . . . And the sounds of the Earth were very interesting to God. And He said "I do so love My Earth." He went on listening. And while God was hearing all these sounds and looking up each one in its own place, He heard one small high sound that called through and over all the others. And God tried to find out what was this weeny sound, but it was hard to find.

Every evening I kept up my "weeny sounds" and my Ritz cracker meal. I asked God to take away my father's glass and give me my mother's heart, but God didn't do one single thing I asked for, at least right then. Nevertheless, I found contentment in my under-the-table chapel for another three years until my grandmother moved in and the dining room table moved out to make room for her bedroom.

I suppose you could say this was my first crisis. I learned to mourn as this experience slipped away. Still, I never forgot it, nor my four friends. Their voices still echo inside me: Cookie, the good girl who loved rituals like the one we invented under the table; Gawkie, a bad boy, my secret favorite, full of mischief and creativity; Cracker, the curious explorer; and God, who listened for "weeny sounds."

By the time I was six World War II was underway. It made the world feel tentative but it gave me a job: dashing around our apartment to pull down all the thick black shades so the war enemy couldn't see to bomb us. I was helping the war effort, Dad said.

School brought more adventures. My school was only for girls. I knew girls were as smart as boys. Still, I went through a cap gun cowboy phase and dreamed of being a boy. The Lone Ranger was my hero, mostly because of his huge and glorious stallion, Silver, and the music of the William Tell Overture that set my heart thrumming. Though sometimes I seriously doubted my own boldness, I galloped around the apartment anyway, yelling "HI HO Silver, away!"

In the summer we went to a farm where I galloped on a real steed and learned some of life's most vivid and dire lessons. The farm was in upstate New York far from anything city-like—dirt roads, small squat farmhouses dotting a landscape of pasture lands, and a big red barn full of animals I'd only seen in picture books, like horses, cows, bulls, pigs, and chickens, and a lot of hay that made me sneeze. I found new "chapels," like my pony Snowfie's velvety snout and the giant cornfields that whispered back to me as I walked, invisible, through them.

My summer job was to crumple up newspapers and stuff them into the rat holes. The farmhouse where we stayed was so full of holes it whistled. I only knew about city cockroaches—shy and mostly hidden—but rats had no modesty. I'd heard lore about rats gnawing babies. Sometimes at night I heard them scritching so I turned on a light and shouted loudly to let them know it wasn't safe to come out. I worried about my little sisters: Laurie, a toddler and Jeanie, born in June, 1945, with curly hair all over her head. My job kept rats away from my sisters.

The war affected life on the farm, too. Farmer Kurtie ran the dairy farm with his wife Ba. Kurtie had come from Germany—Hamburger, I'd thought. Some official people came and confiscated his radio. It was Kurt who persuaded my father not to enlist because he had a family.

"Aren't you happy you don't have to be a soldier, Daddy?" I asked.

"Well, yes," he said, but he didn't smile.

"Would you like a martini?"

"No, thanks," he said then stooped to my level. "But how 'bout a hug?"

Bella, Kurt's and Ba's daughter, was just my age. When we were old enough, we got to ride out on our ponies and herd the cows from their field back to the barn for milking—another important job. Once I saw a pregnant cow sink in quick mud and disappear—completely gone. Another time I watched a cow deliver her calf, a girl Kurtie named Lynnie after me. That slimy knee-buckled calf walked too early yet she made it to her mother. I swear the mother and baby kissed with their noses.

Another time I watched surgery on a cow's stomach for hardware retrieval and learned I could faint. Bovine sex, however, was by far the most harrowing farm lesson, one I should have fainted over. But I'd wanted to see a male cow, a bull, so my mother brought me to the barnyard where I stood up on the fence for the best view. This was one time when my insatiable curiosity did not pay off, through no fault of the bull. The cow stood chewing her cud, heedless of the creak of the barnyard door and the large bull trotting out. Bulls were supposed to be fierce and snort but this one didn't seem ferocious, as he angled over to the cow and climbed up on her back side of all things. She raised her head and let out an ear-splitting bellow as the jouncing bull dangled from her haunches.

"What are they *doing*, Mommy?"

Right then and there, my mother seized the moment and told me all about human sexual intercourse in detail, finishing up with the astonishing disclaimer, "And Lynnie, this is the most beautiful thing a man and a woman do together. It's love." Mom said many odd things but that was the most insane. My father would not do such a thing. Sex, I decided, would not be my preferred route to maturity; nor would trusting my mother much, especially after she told me I couldn't watch her and Daddy do it.

Horses, I felt sure, were above sex. They were the most powerful, holy creatures God could ever have made. One of my most enduring memories of the farm was riding breakfasts. Bella and I, the two oldest daughters, rode out with our fathers into the open country predawn. The image engraved on my heart is this: my father and I sitting still and quiet, I on my small pony and he on his big horse—together like one, our souls riveted as we watched the globe of orange sun rise and take over the earth for a new day. After that we ate breakfast sandwiches Mommy had made of bacon slathered with mayo and a shred of lettuce—unhealthfully delicious and with no cocktails. Sometimes we'd end up at the swimming hole and ride our horses bareback into the cool water. I didn't know horses could swim, but Snowfie slipped into the water and glided along like magic. I gripped his mane with both fists until I understood that I had to trust his strength, not mine.

The summer I was to turn eight I had a strange experience. I was sitting in jodhpurs on the edge of my bed removing my riding boots. I smelled of barn: scents of stable dung, hay, and oats, all mixed together. I closed my eyes: I could sense Snowfie's nose quivering to my kiss and feel the warm exhale of his snort; I could hear the clink of the bridle as it came off and he tossed his head, spraying me with saliva that he licked off my hands. When I opened my eyes I saw only the thin curtain flutter, lifted by a hot stale swish of summer air. Watching thoughtlessly, I suddenly felt saturated with a feeling of inexplicable well-being. It lasted seconds and felt eternal. No matter how hard I tried I couldn't make it happen again.

I decided right then that when I got back to city school and entered third grade, my art project would be an illustrated version of The Lord's Prayer, which I'd memorized in Sunday School. I spent the rest of that summer planning my project: God's sandals would be difficult but I'd get help, then use a lot of gold and glitter for GOD, a name so unique no human had it. *Thy will be done* was a puzzle because God had never exactly told me what it was. Jesus, I'd heard in church, was God, but he hadn't made it into this prayer—probably because he was encased in stained glass and preoccupied with far too many clingy children, a few of them girls. I took Jesus out of the window and drew him into my prayer, with an outsized halo and surrounded by a bunch of stick figure kids, some with triangle-shaped skirts—on earth as it is in heaven.

I knew I wasn't a good artist, but it didn't seem to matter much.

CHAPTER 2 The Old God-Man

M y home altar is a low table in front of which I kneel daily to whine, plead, babble, keep silence, read, and give thanks. It is covered with spiritual tchotchkes, each one carrying its own meaning. Two pictures carry special meaning for me. Both stood in places of prominence in many family homes before they got to my altar.

A three-year-old girl looks out from a small oval rose-adorned frame, her serious gaze daily reminding me to remember her under the table. Next to her stands a photo of the same girl at eight, her dark brown hair tucked behind her ears, tumbling over her shoulders. A beretta-like choir cap perches on the back of her head; bangs cascade over her forehead. Her choir robe is topped by a shoulder cape tied with a crooked bow. In her right hand she holds a tilting electric candle; her left hand, clutches sheet music; but her eyes glance to her right.

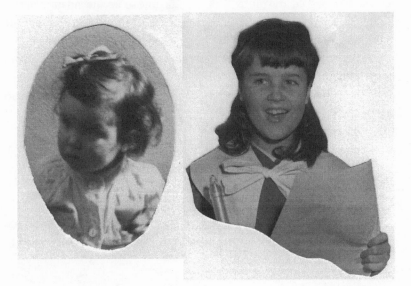

My mother cherished both photos. The small one she kept at her bed-side; the other one made the living room mantel. It first appeared in the Christmas Eve edition of the *New York Herald Tribune* in 1946. In it I'm standing with the children's choir on the steps of the Brick Presbyterian Church. My mother got a copy and had my father cut away the background figures so she could place me alone in a round stand-up gilt frame.

More interested in maternal pride than in church, Mom thought I was an *angel*. But I was no angel, just one among many child singers, all lungs for the birth of a special baby named Jesus who loved us, we knew, because the Bible said so, along with just about every hymn we sang. I wasn't so sure about Jesus as the *only* son, but I'd come to believe that Jesus loved kids like God did so I sang with all the power my alto voice could summon. Some-times I'd wish I were a soprano because they were so loud. Miss Ball, our school's music teacher, said all voices were important and sopranos should blend. They were show-offs, I thought.

Christmas was coming and the war was over—no more black shades or bombs. I could look out of the clear windows and see city people below almost bouncing instead of trudging along. Everything was happy.

I'd seen pictures of dancers called the Rockettes in the newspaper. These lady dancers stood in a straight line and moved their legs all at once, so they looked like a string of paper dolls cut from a single piece of paper that when you shook it out there they were all strung together. The Rock-ettes were precision dancers, the latest big-city phenomenon. I read that they could kick over their heads and change costumes like lightning, some-times forty times in one show. To keep up their stamina they ate chocolate and other sweets and never had to go on a diet.

"Daddy, can we go to the Rockettes?" I begged. "Look at their legs."

"Pretty amazing," he said.

"Yes, but can we go?" I persisted. "My legs might be like Mommy's some day."

"Well, we'll see, Lynnie," he said.

I felt pretty.

I often wondered if he suggested the Rockettes excursion to my aunt, who soon invited me to go as a Christmas treat. It was like him to do a thoughtful thing like that when he wasn't attached to his martini glass.

Radio City Music Hall was enormous and filled with children whose usually immodest voices were hushed. *You would love this*, I whispered to God. We sat in row fifteen. I counted the rows to pass time, and hardly no-ticed the man who took the aisle seat to my left. Out of the corner of my eye,

I glimpsed his long white beard, sleek and silky—like God's, not Santa's. The curtain slowly slowly rose and the lights dimmed. I was spellbound. It wasn't long before I felt the old man's hand on my left leg. He began to caress it softly, going further up every time I took his hand away, further up under my brand-new green-and-purple dirndl skirt.

What is he doing?

I knew this was bad, but my skin tingled with pleasure. At the same time I felt paralyzed with terror. I felt as if I had no power and no voice at all. All that moved was my left hand, which like a robot removed his hand—over and over and over.

I never saw the Rockettes.

Going home in the taxi, my aunt gushed about the the show. I listened carefully so I could tell my mother all about it. I couldn't tell her I'd missed the Rockettes, because I'd seen the bearded old man in the lobby after the show and his fierce beady eyes caught my gaze, paralyzed me the way his touch had, and gave me a message: *don't ever tell.* The other reason I didn't tell was that a new and sharp feeling clutched my gut. It was shame, not the same as hot cheeks and a blush in school if I got the wrong answer, but a full-body blush that didn't go away.

City buses hissing and taxi horns beeping no longer had their usual lullaby effect as I tried to sleep that night. I might have had visions of lovely ladies' legs and dreamed them right onto my grown-up dream body. Instead, I felt the old man's touch. I tried to pray but it felt wooden. All that came out was a dutiful blessing list, then amen. My thumb was still attached so I sucked it raw and finally, finally dozed off. In the morning I no longer felt the old man's touch but I couldn't stop thinking about him. My mind demanded that I make sense of this horror; it searched for some place to land and found a memory. I'd overheard my mother say to my father, "What's wrong with that child? She never says hello to the doorman, dear sweet man. Every morning she just walks on by." My father gave no answer.

Being nasty to the poor doorman was just my way of trying to be me, and not my mother's project—perfect and never quite right. Mom's comment was a thing of the past by three years and nothing unusual for any frustrated parent, but my frightened and needy mind seized on it and turned it against my very soul. Something *was* wrong with me. It had nothing to do with the doorman, but it did have to do with the shame I felt because my body had felt something my mind didn't want it to feel. I could no longer get God, my anchor and confidante, to tune in. My spiritual confusion hurt almost worse than self-condemnation because, you see, the old bearded man looked so exactly like my mental image of God. My mind named him the old god-man.

Rationalization is a very poor substitute for the whole truth, but what frightened eight-year-old knows that?

What happened to me? What is wrong with me?

In silence I yearned and hoped my parents would ask or guess that something had happened. I couldn't tell God about it because God, I believed, had betrayed me. The child in the framed photo was far away. I hung my dirndl skirt in the closet where it would stay till I outgrew it. My mother never asked about it. So I focused on something else—school, especially music class.

Miss Ball, the music teacher, was tall and had a big voice. She wore her hair curled into a bun covered with an almost-invisible hairnet. I loved her with a childlike adoration verging on envy. Miss Ball had become Mrs. Davis over Christmas that year. Things happen over Christmas. But she looked the same so I was sure she would call on me, as usual, to demonstrate my "whole-throated notes." When I got up to sing, my notes came out squished and ugly. I tried over and over, until finally Miss Ball told me I must have a sore throat and sent me back to my seat. My throat wasn't sore, just locked. This was another humiliation—a public one. My radical voice change, I decided, must be like Miss Ball becoming Mrs. Davis over Christmas—the same person and not. After the old god-man I was the same girl—and not.

Nothing is wrong with me and I will prove it became my solemn vow, and school my ally and proof text. What mattered now was being good at things. Art was out and now music. But theater and languages, even Latin, proved vow worthy. In fact, Nadine Nash Blackwell, the red-haired drama teacher who was only a little taller than me, the shortest girl in my class, starred me in our fourth-grade pantomime play *Cinderella*. She coached me to evoke horror on my face so the audience would know without words that Cinderella had spilled an entire bucket of water while scrubbing and was therefore in grave danger. I could act it without feeling it. I'd rather have memorized lines. Memorization was proof of achievement. Still, I had the lead and mattered to Mrs. Blackwell and my theater buff mother.

School success and best friends kept my soul alive. We best friends felt flawless to each other. Together we were allowed to walk to the movies at RKO 86th Street. On the way home my friend Nancy and I were accosted by a group of girls who pulled our hair and snatched our scarves. We got away and ran ourselves breathless. Even after the girls had given up the chase I kept running. I felt a terror almost as keen as what I'd felt in the theater, but this time I could run, and this time I told, something I later regretted because I thought it might have been a factor in my parents' decision to move to the suburbs, away from the city, where conditions were changing, they said.

We moved to Darien, Connecticut, by the time I turned twelve. Because of social and, I believe, class pressures, my parents also decided that we should summer in Westhampton, Long Island. Twelve is not the best age to move—my school, my city, my friends, my farm, and my pony, all gone. I bet by then I could have taught a whole course in how to mourn without dying of grief—or how to hate your parents and still love them. But I was getting to the age when I had to urgently concern myself with Project Life, which to me meant getting a boy, getting a period, getting some boobs, and getting a best friend—also not bothering God about my plans, or for that matter thinking that God, who never uttered a darn word, was any kind of savior.

I hated Darien, not so much for its social purity, or the fact that, by "gentlemen's agreement," Jews were excluded from buying real estate on its shore, or even because there were embarrassing jokes about "Aryans from Darien" in the Broadway play *Auntie Mame*, but because Darien's country club/cocktail party culture increased Dad's drinking, Mom's anxiety, and my smoldering rage as a late-blooming adolescent tragedy with out-of-control parents and enrolled in a roiling junior high school with boys in it. Most of it was the times, but who knows about the "times" when they're in the middle of those "times"?

Three things saved my life.

(1) Annie, my Darien best friend. She straightened my head out about sex, which turned out to be exactly what my mother had told me, but without barnyard animals. Annie didn't laugh at my embarrassment. "Your mother jumped the gun"—we both thought that was impossibly hilarious— "and scared you shitless. A trauma." I liked this new word *trauma*. "But it doesn't mean you're abnormal. I read about it." When I went home and told my mother that Annie had told me all about sex, she turned and muttered to the air, "I don't understand that girl. I told her about sex years ago." I guessed my mother didn't know much about sex herself, but at least

I was unraveling the knot and could begin my sexual career. All I needed was a boy, blood, and boobs.

(2) The Holy Bible. I read it from cover to cover, night after night, though I only skimmed Leviticus. I was looking for dating advice and the holy book was a bust. God got a girl pregnant, apparently a good thing back then, but not the 1950s when getting pregnant meant scandal and exile. Biblical stories, especially in the Old Testament, were pretty juicy though. People did really bad things; God was moody, even tempermental, like a teenager, yet somehow God and people kept getting back together again, even after the worst sins, disasters, breakups, and traumas, some of them caused by God. The Bible made me laugh but there wasn't a damn thing in there to help me get a period or boobs. I tortured my mother with dramatic laments about being deformed for life. Exasperated, she one day turned on me and almost shouted, "Lynnie, for God's sake shut up, you come from a long line of bosoms. You'll get them!"

(3) Bill Brakeman. I met him at a party, one of those high school, hope-soaked, loosely chaperoned events at the home of an overweight girl whose popularity was enhanced by such parties and the feasts her mother prepared for her friends. In one room a couple spent the whole evening with bodies pressed and shuffling in a movement no one could call a dance. I was in the dining room grazing on celery, longing to gorge on chocolate cake, and imagining myself fat when I saw Bill standing in the corner. He smiled. I smiled. We smiled and exchanged shy "hi's." Bill was swoonishly handsome with dark hair, and a look full of innocent wistfulness. My heart sprang into his.

"Are you here with Beebe?"

"I was, but . . ."

"I'm here alone," I said.

Our conversation proceeded at its teenage halting best.

"Maybe we should hit the Driftwood Diner for a hamburger after the party," Bill said.

"What about *her*?" I said.

"We'll drop her home first. You sit up front," he said.

Bill's plan felt romantic, daring, even scandalous—ditching Beebe after she'd been callous toward him. I hopped into the front seat of his, yes, chartreuse Chevy convertible. We dropped Beebe off then drove to the diner. I felt sorry for her, a little.

The diner served the most succulent hamburgers I'd ever tasted. Ketchup oozed from the bun and my tongue darted out to catch it. I wasn't embarrassed to eat in front of Bill.

"I hate it here," I said.

"This diner?" he said.

"No, this town. I miss my city. This place makes my father drink more than ever."

"My father too. I miss Chicago. But this burger is the best. So are you."

Bill had great wit. His stories joined us in laughter.

"Just after we moved the school had to test me," he told me.

"Yeah, me too," I said.

"You should have seen my mother's face when the test lady called to tell her that I had an IQ status of moronic. No kidding," he said. "She wanted to know how I'd find a lost ball in a field."

"Just head to where it landed and look," I said.

"Of course, but the dumb woman wanted me to start at the edge of the field and circle inwards." We split our sides laughing.

Bill and I became a couple, an "item," to my mother, who was thrilled. I felt happy and safe with Bill, and proud of my emergent boobs. We mattered together. In the teen testing lab called high school, we joined the "middle class"—solidly friendly, not nerds or hoods or cheerleader/football greats or prom kings and queens.

"Darling, it's you," my mother said after we visited Smith College. Dad had lobbied for Vassar because his mother had gone there and was sure I'd get a scholarship. He lost. Mom's support encouraged me to bare a tiny corner of my soul and tell her about the theater trauma.

"By the way, Mom, did I ever tell you what happened to me in the theater when I was eight and went with Aunt Tink to see the Rockettes?"

"No dear, what?"

"This old man molested me by putting his hand up my leg." I stopped there and waited.

"Oh no. How awful. Well, such things happen, perverts you know," she said, and then turned and walked into the kitchen.

My ploy for unlocking her heart hadn't worked. I felt sad. "Such things happen" in fact helped us both avoid the pain of the old man.

At Smith College I was back with girls again. I fell passionately in love with ideas in any field including that of my own mind, and also with a few professors and the madness of weekend beer binges. I'd broken up with Bill, which infuriated my mother, but I wanted to check the pulse of my libido and to have dates at Harvard, Dartmouth, Amherst, my whole narrow little Ivy League world. My heart was set on achieving academic success, but I also worried about marriage, babies, having real sex with orgasms, Bill, and the whereabouts of God. Bill and I, never very far apart, resumed dating. Almost flippantly I suggested I accompany a good friend to Mass. She had to go, she said. Or what? I asked. Sin, she said. So I went to Mass, and bingo!—or more biblically, Behold!—there it was, my under-the-table meal the Holy Eucharist, all laid out for me to remember and relive.

I was riveted watching these worshipers—sitting, standing, making signs of the cross on themselves, walking together up the aisle to kneel at the altar rail, rubbing shoulders, sticking out their tongues to be fed like baby birds. I inhaled sweet incense, listened to murmured Latin, and watched. I noticed a woman up front, too, a statue and bad art but unmistakably female. I secretly imagined that this was how God might worship.

Communion in the Presbyterian Church where I'd grown up had felt lonely. Everyone sat motionless in their pews while trays of neatly cubed bread were passed around, followed by more trays of glass cups, each with a "jigger" of grape juice. It was tidy sacramental individualism.

I wanted my meal and oh, I craved my God.

I took instructions one summer to become Roman Catholic. My mother was so horrified that she invited the priest for dinner. It was her way of overcoming her disgust at rosary-bound piety and her own sister's conversionary zeal. She needn't have worried however, because it wasn't long before I discovered that this church was male with no hope. There was the one stone virginal woman up front, yes, but no room for flesh-and-blood women up front.

Back in college for my senior year I consulted Mr. Unsworth, the handsome college chaplain whom Dad called "pipe smoking and tweedy."

"You have some religious yearning," he said. "I wonder why you didn't major in religion."

"I thought of it but I chose Spanish because I'm good at language and wanted to go deeper into Hispanic literature and culture," I said, omitting mention of the fact that I also had a crush on one of the Spanish professors, an olive-skinned Iberian poet with huge eyes.

"Tell me about your religious background," the chaplain said.

"I fell in love with the Catholic Mass. It was rich and sensory, not like the dryness of the Presbyterian worship I grew up with, but when I took instructions to become Catholic I found out they had too many rules and didn't like women," I said.

"Oh, Protestant too plain and Catholic too tight," he said, with a grin that made me blush. "Have you tried the Episcopal Church? A blend that might suit you. There's a parish right here in Northampton. They have Eucharist at least once a month. Try it, then go talk to their priest, to explore more. Let me know how it goes." He rose and extended his hand. God, he was handsome.

"Thanks," I said, excited that he'd said "priest." This Episcopal Church had priests. How could there be a church that looked Catholic but wasn't? I tried it; their meal was open to all baptized Christians; I qualified. Public kneeling was a first for me. I loved the feel of it. Episcopalians stuck out their cupped hands, not their tongues. Maybe here there was a chance for women who weren't statues to be up front. I was confirmed in my senior year of college by Bishop Robert M. Hatch, who put his hands on my head and invoked the Holy Spirit. I felt small and big at once. How much the blessing of a bishop would come to signify in my life I could not know. At least I didn't develop another crush.

My mother I'm sure was relieved, but it was Dad who was impressed by the confirmation liturgy.

"This was beautiful, Lynda," he said. (He called me my full name when he was seriously impressed or seriously angry.) "Not sure about all the fancy robes, but the Communion all together at the altar was nice."

"That's what I like too Dad," I said. "A little more dressed up than Presbyterians."

"Our dour Scotch blood," he said.

"Scottish, Dad, Scottish."

"I grew up in the Episcopal Church, you know," Mom said. "Daddy and I were married at St. Bartholomew's in New York. This service seemed a little too fancy and Catholic for me." Years later, by the time I was married with children, Dad chose to be confirmed in the Episcopal Church himself. I got the oddest, proudest queasy feeling that he was following me into this church.

College gave me a diploma but no requisite diamond ring. I wasn't ready to "settle down" so I spent the summer in Spain with families in Madrid and Santander. In Spain I inhaled religion—Catholicism on steroids, but I soaked it up. The statue lady came alive. The people worshipped a woman—a woman praised as if she were God, a woman held in high holy esteem, a woman beloved. The Señora in Santander called her family to prayers daily with loud clapping, her hands like small enfleshed shofars. And always we hailed Mary. She after all did precede Jesus! I still pray the Hail Mary in Spanish, the way I learned it.

Make no mistake, patriarchy was alive and well in Spain. The women ran things at home and were emotionally dominant, but the men ran the world—and sex. I attracted the attentions of a few married men, whom I rebuffed, in bad Spanish with a flattered ego, explaining that, in *las USA*, women didn't do such things, which meant that *I* was too scared to do such things.

Paco, the older son in my Madrid family, invited me to go to a bullfight. I feigned disapproval. *Toro, toro, toro, ven, ven, guapa,* he teased, waving his arms and an imaginary cape before me. I went. I was quickly drawn into the heat of the crowd. *Olé* sounded like hosanna. Would I have yelled "Crucify him" in the crowd that turned on Jesus, their hero? A bullfight is no barnyard event. The crowd swayed and moaned and roared as one. My God, this experience was lustful, just like religious mystics wrote about their ecstasies. Great God Almighty, I'm having a public orgasm. Please God let me have one in private, too.

In Spain I smelled holiness, dark and musty in cathedrals. I tasted the blood of ritual sacrifice—raw and unhygienic, like and unlike the sacramental meal I craved. I'd read Cervantes's classic *Don Quijote,* but now its spirit was in my bones despite the fact that I could not decide if I was Don Quijote, foolishly stabbing at windmills and filled with indignation at the ills of the world he believed was transformable, or the squat lumphead peasant, Sancho Panza, loyal to the end and scared to quivering about going against just about anything.

The Episcopal Church had promise, but the ordination of women was like one of Quijote's windmills. I felt spiritually enlarged being part of the 80-million-member Anglican Communion. The 2.2-million-member Episcopal Church had a governance of checks and balances, much like the US government, so power wasn't concentrated in a central authority. It was not a dogmatized institution, yet it had a hierarchical structure and an all-male priesthood. Women could be ordained deacons but not priests. Deacons were canonically restricted to a ministry of service to church and world—which very nearly fit women's traditional social roles.

Why, I wondered, was Eucharist the purview of men only? It was clearly a meal in which God acted like a woman—feeding a gathering around a dining table. I noted that the altar guild, ladies all, set up and cleaned up after the meal presided over by a man. I clung to my love of this meal I felt sure was somehow mine—while writing in my diary about sex and spinster fear and Bill Brakeman.

"Bill Brakeman is such a dear handsome man, don't you think?" my mother, who had taken Bill to lunch while I was in Spain, cooed. Yes, I did think Bill was dear and handsome and I did love him. We'd had this Lindy Hop pattern to our relationship for years, swinging away from each other, nearly losing grasp, then crashing back together so hard I'd feel crushed and pull away again, because of some inner unidentifiable hesitation I didn't understand. Letting go of the security of understanding, I became engaged to Bill. We were a ringed "item" now, quite normal. Under a Danforth fellowship, I taught Spanish at Smith for a year while Bill finished up at RPI. We married in June 1961. My overjoyed mother orchestrated a voluptuous outsized celebration at their Darien home. I wore a plain white unembellished wedding dress.

Now we were married. We could do *it*. It was our sexually legal debut—and we couldn't do *it*. My vagina set up its own "No Admittance" sign. I cried, over-apologized, and together we downed a whole bottle of champagne. The next morning while waiting for our flight to Bermuda I called my mother. It's true, I did.

"Mom," I whispered, cupping my hand over the phone receiver.

"Darling, how are you two lovebirds?" she asked.

"We're not lovebirds," I said.

"What?" she said. "Speak up, I can't hear you."

"We couldn't do *it*," I hissed into the phone.

"You mean . . ." she said.

"Yes, I'm not normal."

"Of course you are darling. Just relax. I remember when Daddy and I were married he was so nervous he poured a whole bottle of champagne down the sink by mistake and ordered a poached egg on toast for dinner in a fancy hotel . . ."

"Okay bye. Have to run catch the plane. Bye." I hung up before she could say one word more.

I told Bill who said, "Thank God we didn't waste *our* champagne." We laughed hysterically at Mom's perverse consolation, which nevertheless worked to relax us, so by the time we got to Bermuda we did *it*. I'd worry about orgasms and any other aspirations later. For now more school. You'd think I'd know who I was by now. My mother did. Bill and I moved into a one-room apartment on the Upper East Side in Manhattan where I attended Columbia University to earn a master's in Spanish while Bill, degreed as an electronics engineer, commuted from New York to Connecticut for his job with an engineering company. My mother selected and installed the drapes for our new apartment. We looked completely normal.

I didn't go to church but I visited some sanctuaries and stared at the magnificent altars at the Cathedral of St. John the Divine and at Riverside Church. I didn't talk to God. I just sat still and knew: an emotional distance had begun to creep into our marriage. We were both introverts, both oldest children, both had dads we loved who drank too much, and both of us were more motivated to succeed alone than together, yet we wanted to be together. We just didn't know how to talk to each other about our fears, resentments, longings, needs, worries, much of anything, but when we drank together we shared freely—up to a point. What we'd talked about that had connected us the night before by morning had vanished. We'd learned our ways growing up in a culture and families where drinking to excess was acceptable, and feelings were less so. We were normal.

I got pregnant while completing my course work at Columbia and we moved back home to Connecticut—to Ridgefield, a town of our own. Bill's mood began to go haywire. For example, he once couldn't locate a book he'd been reading. He accused me of losing his book, called me an asshole, and punched through the cheap plasterboard wall with his fist. This kind of thing only had to happen once or twice before I became sure lots of things *were* my error or fault.

Wrapped in a blanket I piled up notes upon notes to study my compulsive brains out for comprehensive graduate exams, which I took two months before our daughter, Beverley, was born in January 1963. Bill held our baby daughter and gazed into her face with a mixture of fear and adoration. We were parents—normal.

Pregnancy and childbirth put me back in touch with God in new ways. Birthing hurt like hell, but the force of my uterus's natural push felt downright omnipotent—pushing for life, forcing embodied life into the light. I could imagine God's laboring to breath life into a hippo, because that's what eight pounds thirteen ounces of slowly emergent baby girl beauty with heaps of black hair felt like. The body I'd divorced after the old god-man incident did all this. Having children reinforced my own capacity for unfathomable and impossible love, a capacity I'd thought I'd lost.

Another daughter, Jill, was born in fourteen months. In three years a boy, Robert William Brakeman III. Bill's father, who had been orphaned at a young age, felt relieved. His name would live on. We vetoed Bobbie or Billie and his sisters' choices, "Skippy" and "Timmy," and called our son R. B. Then we cast a vote for the American dream and purchased our first home back in Darien, an architectural double of my parents' house, one street over.

All around me the sixties were exploding. I felt itchy inside. But I was not the decider. Bill had a career opportunity in Anniston, Alabama, and we moved, this time far away and into a foreign land. The children adapted and developed thick drawls. I didn't do as well. I drank too much, spent too many hours wielding my new floor waxer around the spacious black-and -white-tiled foyer, helplessly watching black flecks spinning off black tiles onto white tiles. I couldn't remember whether the psalm said you could or could not sing the Lord's song in a foreign land so I went church shopping and discovered the uptown Episcopal parish was segregated and the downtown one was more Baptist than Episcopal.

Bill's boss was a tyrannical boozer who called late one night for Bill to come rescue him from a Birmingham hospital where they were "holding" him for unstoppable hiccups.

"Let the asshole hick himself to death," I said.

"He's my boss," Bill said.

"Well, fire him!" I yelled as he left.

Bill imitated hiccups. We laughed and . . .

The failure of birth control for an "old and tired uterus" (quote from the doctor) brought wonders: the feeling of life moving within me once more. Life multiplies life. I am never sure how or why such paradoxical happiness mysteries happen but I suspect it is through some bright combination of divine and human co-creating. In this case, Dad, now retired after a long and successful career, invited Bill to start a business with him—in the Hartford area. We piled into our blue Chevy wagon named Roosevelt Franklin, and headed north—home. I patted my huge belly and told it to wait. John Thomas was born just three days after we arrived—another new town, another new life, another new baby, another new chance.

The 1970s could work.

CHAPTER 3 It Was a Very Good Year—for Cookies

By 1973, we lived in a four-bedroom colonial in North Canton, Connecticut. I relished my children's blossoming lives with affection and some uncertainty. Were we settled? Were we normal yet?

Bill and my father had very different ways. Dad, through Mom, complained to me about Bill's making promises they couldn't keep—ping!—and Bill complained to me that my father was too damn organized—pong! Dad finally decided he couldn't afford to continue and wrote Bill a letter. It was cowardly but it gave Bill some dignity space and opened the way for him to do what he'd always wanted: to start a business of his own.

"So this company I want to buy is in Stratford," he told me.

"Stratford where?" I said.

"Connecticut, Lyn."

"How far away is it?"

"Oh, maybe a hundred miles or so. I can commute till you find us a house down near there."

My halfhearted house search bore the same results as any half-hearted activity. It failed. Bill got an apartment in Stratford, and commuted. I stayed home and watched my children grow. I wanted to grow, too. Bill's energy went into his career, mine into the children. When Bill was home our "mutual affair" with alcohol protected us from ourselves and each other. We drank B & L scotch, a brand we affectionately dubbed "Bill & Lyn's."

My prayers had become dusty and dull but the local parish, Trinity in Collinsville, needed volunteers—for everything. Getting involved soothed my longings somewhat. What did I want? I was doing everything expected, I thought, yet I sat in my suburban kitchen baking chocolate chip cookies, a righteous activity that felt clumsy, and dreamed of a job with a paycheck. I reached for the necessary baking ingredients, one by one, from the refrigerator, pantry, and cupboard. In a dreamily narcissistic moment, I noticed my wrist—delicate, lovely, slim. It might, I imagined, have belonged to Princess Grace or a saint or mystic like Dame Julian of Norwich, of whom I'd dimly heard. Just gazing at my wrist caused me to realize—how long had it been, years? —that I scarcely noticed lovely things about myself.

The images of children who would delight in my cookies dashed across my mind's eye. Bev, ten, a dark beauty who stalked me—her presence closer than my shadow, her gaze intense, seeming to question my right to exist. Jill, nine, also beautiful, with delicate features and an audacious mountain of curls to match her chutzpah. She had issued her declaration of independence at four—"There's just not enough air in the world for me and Bev!" R. B., six, his face bright, irresistibly pleasing, plaintive, and lightly shadowed with anxious bewilderment. John, maturely handsome for a two-year-old, had a beguiling timidity that camouflaged the inner turmoil of his own miniature life in the shadow of three big siblings.

"Lynnie, the highest destiny for any woman is to be a good mother." Mom's fail-safe prescription for happiness sounded to me like a proscription. I had followed her rules but questioned myself mercilessly. Was I a good enough mother? Why didn't I have orgasms? Very little made me angry. But I went to church. All was well.

All is not well at all. Something is wrong with me.

I had a secret and it wasn't the old god-man. My secret was a broken heart. It was so broken that half of it fell out that day in my kitchen over cookies.

Why are you doing this?

An inaudible voice inquired, a polite, curious voice of simple candor and blinding clarity. It wasn't my voice; it was, well, not from my mind. The only thing about this voice that was like me was that it asked a question. I scurried around the kitchen, ordered the utensil drawer, rearranged the canisters on the counter, and was about to go for the vacuum cleaner when I crumpled, sat down, put my head on the kitchen table, and sobbed.

How did you know, God?

The God who had listened to me as a child had found a voice. Jolted out of my spiritual torpor, I followed the cookie voice and waded into the deep turbulent waters of my self—looking for me, looking for God, looking for purpose, life, sex, and meaning beyond motherhood.

23

Before I embarked on an unknown path, I knew I should have a clean house. I grabbed the vacuum as if to throttle it and buzzed it around. When you're making a decision you know will go against everything your mother, the church, and the world has set up for you, things get messy. In fact, when you listen to God from your soul's depths, plan on dissonance. I was scared alive.

I seized life, grabbed for it, slashed wildly at what felt like a large thick oxygen-depriving plastic bag all round me. I rushed from Eden's safety, apple in hand. This path of disobedience felt obedient to me, "meet and right" as the liturgical prayer said. One of the first things I did was to have an affair with a man, a flirty fling that upped my aliveness. It might not have been God's will, but it was mine. Who can ever know what God's will is, anyway? All I knew was that God had asked me a good question.

My next action was to enter bioenergetic therapy. That was just after I'd smashed the small aqua sugar bowl, that went with the aqua-and-white set of everyday dishes, which didn't go with the two-tone persimmon-and-copper kitchen, onto the kitchen table. It shattered into more pieces than Humpty Dumpty. Sugar mixed with chunks and chips of cheap porcelain fanned out over the table as four astonished faces, with spoons filled with Cheerios poised on the way to hungry mouths, looked up. This was not their mother. Silence as heavy as a dentist's X-ray apron slapped down on us all. A couple of tears rolled down John's cheeks and more than a couple down mine. Bev got up and began to pick the broken shards from the sugar. Jill went to fetch her Siamese cat, and R. B. helped Bev, and said, "It's okay, Mom."

"You're getting in touch with your anger," my new counselor said. He was handsome, bearded, and a Rev. named John. He explained bioenergetic therapy, the brainchild of Alexander Louwen, as body work with deep breathing based on the idea that all the emotions one has ever felt were stored in the muscles. Emotions seek release. Of course!

"You mean my muscles could mess up my happiness, make me smash sugar bowls and scare my kids?" I asked.

"Well, not your muscles exactly, but the unresolved feelings trapped in your muscles. We'll take it slowly, and talk about everything," John assured me.

"You're seeing a psychiatrist, now?" my mother asked. "What ever for?"

"I feel fucked up inside," I said.

"Lynnie, that's just ridiculous," she proclaimed.

I bought a pink leotard and joined a bioenergetics exercise group after I'd stored up my fear in some muscle or other. I followed the instructions with care when suddenly I noticed, out of the corner of my eye, a woman collapse, curl up, and begin to suck her thumb. I kept breathing vigorously and tried not to gawk, or panic.

"I'm not sucking my thumb," I told John, but didn't tell him I'd sucked my thumb till I was twelve.

"Don't worry, Lyn," he said. "I know this woman and she was returning to her early comfort zone. She won't stay there. You get in touch slowly."

What in God's name would I be "in touch with" next? I grew to detest that concept, but John seemed trustworthy. Some people, I'd heard, worked in the nude or underwear, so the therapist could see the muscles. Would I do that? I lost weight in case. Backbending over a stool released a welter of sorrow hidden under my breastbone. In my original family I'd cried at Christmas when everyone else was happy trimming the tree. I'd cried because Dad wasn't there or was drunk, which my mother called "tired"; I'd cried because I'd broken my mother's happiness rule, I'd cried because I felt different and somehow wrong. In therapy I didn't suck my thumb or talk about the old god-man in the theater, but my body again asserted itself against my will, this time for my good.

Act III was to turn into Brenda Starr, girl reporter. I became a stringer, paid by the column inch, writing for a regional newspaper. My first paycheck was frameable, but I spent it. My byline thrilled me: "Planning and Zoning Commission Labors Over Decision to Close Town Dump" by Lyn Brakeman. Town meetings bored me stiff until I got home, poured myself a scotch, sat down at the dining room table with my typewriter, and wrote as many inches as I could, trying to infuse drama into tedium. My mother and my children did more babysitting than was good for any of them, a fact for which I remain grateful—and slightly guilty.

The Episcopal Church was as astir with change as I was. Right after my kitchen epiphany the church voted *against* a resolution to make it possible for women to be ordained priests. As a result, many women and some men restarted the life of the church, in ways about as untidy as mine. Women were raising hell, for the sake of heaven. Rules more ancient and entrenched than my, or even my mother's, ideas of propriety, would be broken to force the church out of its torpor. If it couldn't be done through proper channels, then it would be done outside canon law, outside God's law too, some thought. Women took independent action and invaded the priestly caste. Would the church repent? Would I?

The Episcopal Church and I began our midlife crises together.

Free, wild, and frightened, I sat in the pew at my parish church and started to wrestle hard with my faith. What, besides God, did I believe in? I stared at the altar meal, my under-the-table meal, seeing it again as if for the first time—this time in a church that was willing to wrestle hard with women.

In the same year the church voted women's ordination out, they voted that lay people (not just male ones) could be chalice bearers. Women were also permitted to read the Sunday Bible readings, and serve on parish vestries. I signed up for everything.

Being a chalice bearer required serious physical discipline just to hold the chalice steady for sips without emptying it down some woman's cleavage while she knelt, her pious head bowed and the brim of her large hat making her lips un-locatable. It took more skill, in fact, than to scoot wee wafers into cupped fists as the priests did. Feeling a little like one of the Great Wallendas, I donned a black cassock and a long white-winged surplice over it. Such a pinafore! Thus I began a ministry *inside* the altar rail of God's dining room table. I gripped that chalice for dear life.

Most astonishing among the expansive changes the church was enacting, was the new wording of the catechism defining ministry. The "ministers of the church" were formerly defined as "bishops, priests, and deacons"—the ordained. Now, the ministers of the church were "lay persons, bishops, priests, and deacons"—hierarchy radically reordered on paper. It meant that baptism, not ordination, made a person a "minister," a status prophesied by a T-shirt slogan of the women's ordination campaign: "Ordain Women or Stop Baptizing Them!"

The Episcopal Church prided itself on its changelessness—a characteristic it ostensibly shared with God. But now, many parts of its touted tradition were becoming unrecognizable: prayers, hymns, the definition of "minister." Would the gender of clergy follow? Would the final staple of the Episcopal security system fall away? The pace of change was so swift that many good folks felt the wind knocked out of their souls. They often sought safety and comfort in resistance. Though many felt qualms about women at the helm, at heart they needed a reassuring mother.

The Eucharist, already rich in sacramental beauty and a reenactment of my childhood spirituality, became charged with new meaning for me. I'd recognized divine womanliness in the preparation and serving of this meal, but now saw that God fed people with her [sic] own body and blood. How much more intimate and nourishing could you get? The holy blood of Christ was less like martyrs' blood or blood spilled by young men in wars, and more like the blood of life spilled by women for fertility. Maybe the patriarchal church had the divine gender wrong?

I kept my ideas to myself, but I began to wonder if this meal was a very different kind of sacrifice than the one proclaimed in the prayers of consecration week after week: *We remember his death, we remember his death*—his bloody, awful death. What about Jesus' life? Did Jesus die for me? I had no answers that worked, and I felt crazy-confused, so I stopped thinking. Still, I couldn't help but wonder if I would die for my children. Likely I would, but I knew for sure I had bled to give them life, and that this Eucharist had more to do with life than death—just as it had for me when I'd invented it under the table.

Next, I began to see Eucharist as a meal of justice: everyone was welcome, everyone got food, everyone got the same, not too little, not too much. One Sunday I sat and watched as everyone streamed up the aisle to kneel side by side at the altar rail, rubbing shoulders and extending their hands to receive their just portion of holy food. It wasn't a dole. It seemed a miracle, because many of these same people had been quarreling vigorously all week about the rector's latest decision, his tenure and sermons, the hymn choices, on and on. The Eucharist brought justice and with it peace—until Monday.

The church needed to be like its meal. Women weren't getting justice. We should be behind altars, not just lecterns, preaching in pulpits, not just making announcements from the pew, distributing bread, not just wine. Caught up in the whirlwind of this transformative era and fed by the Eucharist, my spirit soared with feminist visions. For me the ordination of women was less about baptismal rights and more about sacramental justice: *all* sacraments, including the sacrament of ordination, should be open to *all* people. There was precedent for this in early church history, though I hoped there would be no bloodied martyrs this time. Jesus' blood was enough, and, by this time, I was sure bloodshed of any kind was not ordained by God. I was equally sure that there was something we should do to help besides bleed. The church which I'd thought was, well, just spiritual, was about to be shaken. I wanted to be passively passionate and stand on the sidelines, but political action, which made me dizzy, was unavoidable.

In 1974 a group of eleven women were ordained priests outside of canon law in Philadelphia, a headline-making scandal. By 1975 four more women were "illegally" ordained in Washington, D.C. Through this movement, well organized and lobbied, women began to hold the church accountable more forcefully than ever. Outside the church too, women were holding society accountable. Amazing reversals were happening. My own state elected Ella Grasso as its first woman governor.

Many people reacted to the newly ordained women priests with verbal venom and hatred. The Washington ordinations nearly didn't happen because of a bomb scare. Bomb-sniffing dogs were brought in before the service began. The Rev. Lee McGee, one of the Washington ordinands, later told me she'd imagined being in the sanctuary before the ordination service quietly praying for her new vocation. "I never thought I'd be praying for my life," she said. To get ordained a woman priest had become a justification for mass murder? We could all be blown up! Was this only the lunatic fringe, or were women truly hated?

The courageous women who pioneered this movement had help from bishops who provided support and ordained them. The bishops were retired but still had authority to perform sacramental acts. Hence, the "rogue" ordinations were sacramentally legitimate, yet politically "illegal," occurring *before* the assembled church officially voted to change the canon law. The "mind of the church"—a phrase conveniently used to postpone action forever—was not yet settled, and women were the disrupters. I couldn't imagine myself going out on such a limb and risking alienation from something as big and powerful as Mother Church, to say nothing of the God people called "Father."

A chilling quote was running around the grapevine of wrath. Carter Heyward, one of the Philadelphia Eleven priests, had received a vile letter after her ordination: "Go to hell, buck teeth! Someone ought to kill you. You're filthy." By now I'd read Betty Friedan's *Feminine Mystique* and was a newly minted feminist who believed that the personal was political, and that the most offensive slurs were comments about a woman's body and looks. How ironic, since women continued to devote so much time, money, and energy to self-beautification, in order to attract positive male attention. How many unnecessary diets had I tried? Thank God I'd already had braces.

The God I'd met in my childhood book and under the table was a God who shone favor on girls, and listened to me. My spirituality was intimately linked to my gender. I was one of three daughters in a family; my first school was founded and headed by a woman; all my teachers were women and all my classmates were girls. The patriarchal church and world in which I lived was crumbling, but my theological foundations held as I wondered how God felt about such desecration of women priests, such vehement rejection of half of *His* image, yet everyone I asked admitted God had no gender. Some people shouted out that what it said in Genesis about God's image being created both male and female didn't count, because it was in the *Old* Testament. In my mind, *He* placed God into one of those genders. Oh yes, but *He* really meant both, we all knew. Perhaps it was then that I began to think of God's putative non-gender in a serious way, and to cringe about the obvious fact that while the heavens proclaimed the glory of God, all the damn English pronouns quietly and consistently proclaimed the infallible masculinity of God. It made me angry.

Ironically, the church's inexorably male God language was so incongruent with the God I'd experienced that becoming a woman priest actually looked like the most congruent action to take. Should I reposition my Ritz-cracker "eucharist" from under the table to where it belonged—on top of the table, an altar where I would preside? Was anger a proper stimulus for a holy vocation? Yes. Anger had motivated me as a child and led me to God. Anger was behind the cries of women for justice, the moves to get ordained before the official vote to ordain, and on their T-shirts. I loved the one that read "God Is Not a Boy's Name." I thought of buying it but didn't.

I wasn't ready to be good yet. I felt like a woman in heat, howling inside like a cat. I lost more weight. I loved feeling hot and joyfully out of control and kept the moral incompatibility of my sexual fantasies and my lofty religious aspirations safely in the inanimate pages of a journal. Hungry for both sexual *and* sacramental intimacy, I tried but couldn't separate these two urgings. Both drove me onward, and both felt inevitable. Hearing nothing from God and, frankly, not praying for restraint, I flirted ruthlessly with the sheer joy of life itself, with men wherever I encountered them, while at the same time dreaming of presiding at the Eucharist.

My therapist cheered my growth spurt and made no judgments, so I fell in love with him, to no avail. Vocational thoughts intruded in strange but recognizable ways. Motherhood, I told myself, was like priesthood. For over ten years I'd preached, taught, celebrated, fed, bathed, and blessed four young lives. I dreamed of going to seminary.

The blond parish rector, one of my flirtees, said one day: "You're attracted to the things of the altar. Have you ever thought of being a priest?"

"No." I lied.

Did this rector, named Steve, know what was inside me? I grew up trying to escape mother's eagle eye and trusting only God to see through me, but this man's spiritual eyesight caught me off guard. I laughed at him, reminding him that the mind of the church wasn't settled.

"It will be," he said.

"I have to become a woman before I can become a woman priest. I don't feel ready and seminary is expensive."

"Just a thought." He shrugged and smiled. "Forget it."

His comment was like telling a jury to disregard some crucial piece of evidence. I could not forget it.

Most people thought that women's ordination would be approved at the 1976 General Convention. A revised edition of the Book of Common Prayer was in the works, as was a hymnal revision. I hoped the committees would make gender language more inclusive, and that they'd excise "Onward Christian Soldiers" from the hymnal—until a woman told me that as a young child regularly abused by her mother, she'd marched around carrying a broomstick cross, a little soldier singing for Jesus. "It gave me courage," she said.

I wanted courage. God had asked me a question, and so had the rector of my parish.

"Were you serious about my being a priest?" I asked him.

"Mmmhmm." He looked up from his desk and smiled all his charm my way.

"What would it take?" I asked.

I tried to concentrate on the details of the ordination process he explained, but his hair got in the way, a shock of blond hair that kept tumbling down onto his forehead. Fascinated, I watched him toss it back in place.

"You first have to become a postulant, as soon as the church votes, and it will. That means the bishop and his committees discern a call to priesthood in you and deem you fit to go to seminary. Lyn, are you listening?"

"Sure."

"Well, what do you think?

"I think I'm scared the committee will ask me too many questions about my personal life."

(I also think I could be falling in love with you.)

"Don't worry. Pray about it and let me know. You'd be a good priest."

(Would I be a good lover?)

I didn't pray. I called Yale Divinity School and made an appointment for an interview and a visit. Just to see. Just in case. My father had graduated from Yale University in 1933. The idea of being a Yalie enticed me. Commuting was feasible. My children were growing up. What if . . . ?

The Yale Divinity School campus is rectangular. Marquand Chapel stands on a rise at the center, surveying the campus from on high and calling faithful worshipers into its bosom of praise. Red brick, white trim, a parade of steps up either side of the entrance to the simple white door, a clock tower with a cross on top—nothing like most Episcopal churches built of stone and with a steeple. It startled me at first. It looked like the Brick Presbyterian Church of my childhood. I was home.

Before I went to my appointment, I entered the chapel's open doors and sat in a white pew. Wordless for once, I listened to my heart speak— thumpety thump—into the silence. God bless me, I said again and again and signed myself with a cross—head, genitals, right breast, left breast— a very full-bodied, un-Protestant thing to do, but an action that solicited God's help to align conflicting forces within. I simply whispered, "God, let me come here."

CHAPTER 4 Set. Breathe. Ready. Go.

In the summer of 1976 the General Convention of the Episcopal Church voted to approve what had already been proved in 1974 and 1975—that women could be priests. I knew this would happen. I'd dreamed of this, but now it was real and upset my efforts at denial.

I heard from some women priests who were at the convention that the atmosphere in which the gathered church, wrapped in awesome silence, had waited for the 1976 tally to reveal whether or not the ordination of women in all three Holy Orders had been explicitly approved, which was tantamount to a Yes vote on women priests, was electric. It was a dramatic, historic, hope-driven *temps vierge* moment of absolute openness when everything or nothing could happen—and change lives forever. The final tally: the clergy order, 114 votes cast, 58 votes needed for affirmative action, Yes, 60; No, 39; Divided, 15. In the lay order, 113 votes cast, 57 needed for affirmative action, Yes, 64; No, 37; Divided, 12. The motion passed. Even as I reread these statistics, I can feel my own tears prickling.

Church unity, perilously threatened by the 1974 and 1975 illegal ordinations, had remained shaky, but now its purpose, which was to cover up the truth for the sake of "peace," fell away completely to reveal what was really upheaved: *male* unity. Some men had betrayed the old boys' club compact. In time I'd understand more about this shattering, but for now all I knew was that women rejoiced and I was voted in. You would have thought it was an ecclesiastical tsunami the way some people carried on about Jesus choosing only male disciples, therefore . . . . Still, the Episcopal Church, normally a snail of an institution, had beat the United States government that had just (1977) defeated the Equal Rights Amendment. Women could be priests. All we had to do was pass their tests, proving there was *nothing wrong with us.* I breathed to my belly as bioenergetics had taught me, puffed out my chest, stood sturdy on both strong legs, and decided to follow these brave women who were making history by overturning the church's man-on-top arrangements.

"Okay, I'm ready to do it," I told the rector.

"Do what?" he said with a grin.

(Seduce you.)

"Be a priest."

"Okay. Wonderful. How come?" he asked.

"You asked," I said.

"And the church voted. I'll inform the vestry. I know they'll sign off on you. So will the bishop. Then you'll go before Committee One to be screened for postulancy. Here, take this ordination manual home and read it."

This manual was a weighty book. Books keep me alive; I'd first seen God in a book. Hugging the manual, I headed home, read it in spurts, and almost backed out.

Requirements for ordination were painstakingly comprehensive: physical examination, interview with a shrink, standardized psychological testing, three screening committees, an interview with the bishop, canonical written and oral exams, ordination as a transitional deacon, and then, in six months if you were still breathing, ordination as a priest. There was a standard of learning: demonstrate proficiency in theology, Bible, liturgics (worship), preaching, pastoral care and counseling, church history and patristics (study of early Church Fathers, no mothers named), ethics and moral theology, polity (church governance,) fieldwork in a parish, and anything else you had time for.

My God, I hoped seminary didn't have many of its own requirements. The job of a parish priest, the expected career track, carried tonnage: leader of a congregation bearing full authority and power over every scrap of community life: administrative, liturgical, instructive, pastoral. Could I do all that?

Who did they think we were, men? Roman Catholic "fathers" weren't married, but we Episcopalians had big fat lively sex lives. All I'd wanted was the sacraments. Women with all this power and authority could upend centuries of conditioning. In my mind's eye I saw myself as a small three-year-old striding off to find the right place for herself.

I entered the ordination process in 1977, feeling legitimate, not like an "issue," yet also not knowing that the bishop of Connecticut at the time had voted *against* the ordination of women as priests. Trinity's vestry approved and sponsored me, so the diocese scheduled me for interviews with Committee One, the committee that advised the bishop about granting aspirants the status of postulancy, a status which officially declared an aspirant qualified to be in the track headed for ordination.

The morning of my screening day, my mind woke up in a traffic jam. Who would be on this committee? What should I wear? There was nothing in the manual about dress code. My mother would say, "Be presentable, darling." I surveyed my closet for what seemed like centuries and selected a black cotton dress with a safe square neckline. Neither Mom nor Mother Church would find slacks presentable.

Dressed presentably, a short, dark-haired woman of thirty-nine, mother of four children, and aspirant to the ordained priesthood, I stood in front of an immense stone retreat house where Committee One met. On the lawn I saw a large statue of the "holy family," mom, dad, infant son—an image the church adored. I should fit in well here. The hot July sun kissed my face. I blew a kiss back and entered the building.

It was Friday afternoon. We six aspirants, four "older" women, above thirty and just below fifty, and two "younger" men, looking like boys, took our places with six committee members, a fair-game clergy-lay mix, all looking very much older, if not in years then in churched-ness.

After introductions, we discussed the assigned book, Graham Greene's *The Power and the Glory*. The old Mexican reprobate alcoholic priest protagonist of Greene's novel was hardly a model for us to imitate. The question to consider: Did the condition of a priest who administered sacraments affect, for good or ill I presumed, the grace of the sacrament? The answer: Of course not. God, on *His* perfectly pronouned own, worked the grace angle independent of human effort. I wondered if this choice of reading was meant to stave off any gender bias accusations—a woman couldn't pollute the sacrament any more than the Mexican drunk, could she?

The Episcopal "cocktail hour" consisted of dry sherry, crackers, and cheese. Lo and behold! The crackers they served were Ritz. I ate exactly five. I have no recollection of dinner. I went to bed early. July aside, I pulled the covers up to my neck and shivered with dread. The crucifix on the wall threw shadows, its cross pieces forming an arrow shape—sharp. I turned away, feeling suddenly so, so sorry for Jesus—and myself.

The next day each aspirant had an hour-long interview with each committee member. A bell rang to signal the next interview. Committee

One members were neatly dressed, men in their clerical collars, women in linen skirts, high-necked blouses, stockinged feet, low-heeled pumps, and basic pearls. They all looked cool.

"Good morning, Lyn," the laywoman with tightly curled graying hair greeted me warmly and folded her hands onto her lap. "I think it's fair to tell you that I am against the ordination of women, although of course that will not interfere with my ability to screen women fairly." I admired her pathology. Ding!

🏃

"How many children do you have, Lyn?"

"Four."

"Well, that's two-point-two-four too many. Their ages?"

"Fourteen, thirteen, nine, and about to be seven. They are wonderful..." I gushed maternal praises.

Where did he get his stats? The Rev. Reginald Winthrop Pugh III was short, frail for his name, with large glasses and a pointy nose sloped like a carrot on a snowman. He was a gay priest. (Everyone knew and no one told.) Which one of my children would he have me assassinate? Ding!

🏃

"Who will supervise your children while you study and while you take on the duties of a priest, assuming of course that you make it through this process?" asked another primly suited laywoman inquired with raised eyebrow, trying to look as if her question was genuine and she expected a real answer. I told her my mother would help out and wondered if this were a screening for priests or mothers. Ding!

🏃

The Rev. Charles Youngsterman had been around the church a very long time, his fingers in about every aspect of its life. "My dear, I liked your essay on vocation and vision. However, you have written about a model of priesthood you call supplemental. We don't have that here. In Connecticut we ordain rectors for parishes."

"Oh, I want to be a rector, definitely. But I thought we were writing a vision. Couldn't there be some priests not in full-time paid parish ministry who could help parish clergy out from time to time but work outside the church proper in pastoral ministries?" Ding!

(Much later I discovered that my model had precedent. Worker priests had at one time been ordained in the Roman Catholic Church and sent into the field to do pastoral care with workers on the docks in Marseilles. The movement worked well until bishops called the priests "home" to parishes, under the watchful eye of their diocesan bosses. Too much extra-parochial priestly activity could get out of control. I didn't realize it then, but I was describing the eventual shape of my own priesthood.)

🏃

Mrs. W. was a social worker with a kind face, fine smile, and fret wrinkles smudged into her skin, hair graying, light dancing in her eyes, a little foxy, a little sugary, a little steely, like a granny. Appearances soothe. I decided she was my ally. Until she spoke.

"Are you happy?"

What kind of question was that? I choked. "Yes, very."

"I was just wondering if ordination would make you happy? You're well qualified and will make a fine priest—in ten years after your children no longer need a mother." Ding!

🏃

The day got heavier and hotter as I trekked along with the bell. The last interview was with the committee chairman, another gay male priest I'll call the Rev. Etherington Sweetwater because he was sweet in a pursed-lip kind of way. "You know, Lyn, I just keep seeing this dear little seven-year-old, or is he still six, boy, hungry and his mother not home. I can see him as he stretches, unable to open the refrigerator." He sighed, his eyes half closed, smiling as he delivered the death sentence. The last bell of the day sounded like a blaring gong in my ear. Ding!

🏃

In the closing plenary session, I asked, "What if you go to seminary anyway, if you're not a postulant?" A hush fell on the room. Then the Rev. 2.24 declared, "That, unless you don't care about ordination, would be an act of defiance against church authority. You'll hear from the bishop. Any more questions?" Aspirants dismissed. Without a word of goodbye or good luck to each other, we aspirants, looking scalped, departed.

In a blurry rage I drove home to my parish and gave rector Steve hell for not preparing me. He suggested I pray, and I hope I didn't tell him to go to hell. Then I went home and made John open the refrigerator for me.

"Why, Mom?"

"Just open it and I'll give you the biggest hug you've ever had, and a treat."

After two dreadful weeks of waiting, the bishop, who had the definitive say over every step of this process, summoned me to his office, where he told me from behind a three-mile-wide desk, "I'm so sorry, Lyn. I know this will come as a great disappointment to you, but Committee One has not recommended you become a postulant, an assessment with which I concur. They said it would be a dual vocation."

I must have looked blank. He continued. "They meant that you couldn't be a mother and a priest."

I smiled and stared at him. He was the pastoral bishop our diocesan clergy had craved and elected, a charming raconteur with a hearty laugh and a twitch that caused him every few minutes to jerk his head to one side. *Poor man, he looks uncomfortable. He belongs back in a parish.* I screened him without scruple until he twitched and a droplet of perspiration flew from his upper lip.

"Dual vocation? What about clergy fathers?" I blurted.

"They're different," he said.

"They have wives," I said. *Mothers too.* Then I cried. He handed me a tissue, a gesture for which I hated him. I don't remember the rest, except that he added something about a "hunch" he had that this wasn't the right time. Was a hunch like a twitch? This interview was over. Ding!

Damned if I didn't thank him when I left.

Only one of us four aspiring women was accepted—and she provisionally. They sent her for more courses in ethics and worried that she'd been in therapy for fifteen years. "What could you expect for a woman in this sexist church and society?" she later quipped. That woman, the Rev. Joan Horwitt, was the first woman ordained (1979) in Connecticut. Of the other two female aspirants, one went home to re-discern her vocation, having been told that the diocese didn't ordain permanent deacons so she would have to be a priest; the other woman went to seminary and then to another diocese whose bishop, friendly to women's ordination, ordained her.

Then there was me. Doubt and shame peppered with indignation enshrouded me. I'd imagined the church would be, well, nicer. I ruthlessly self-screened, feeling like the biblical Job, who carried on for thirty-seven chapters about how God let the innocent righteous suffer, until God *Himself*, probably fed up, appeared and took Job for a long lovely walk through all creation. Was God showing off, or simply letting Job in on enough of the divine mind to give him a new vision? Neither Job nor God smoothed my doubts; instead they deprived them of their power to possess me completely. I left on our family vacation. I didn't feel motherly that year, so my family mothered me: they left me alone on the beach.

𓃒

I'm toeing soft sand. The large solar globe glares. Alone on the beach in a chair with a towel and my Bible, I flip it open. And there it is: the book of Judith. I shake my head no. This book, God, is apocryphal, like an extra in the theater, interesting but not canonical—like me. But my attention is pulled to Judith's prayer: "O Lord God of my ancestor Simeon, to whom you gave the sword to take revenge on those strangers who had torn off a virgin's clothing, to defile her, and exposed her thighs to put her to shame . . . you said 'It shall not be done'—yet they did it."

𓃒

My God, I felt "raped" by a committee, shamed by prejudices God detested. This Judith was a widow of no account, but a woman who talked to God. She seduced the Assyrian general who was out to destroy her people, then, after he passed out from too much lust and wine, she struck his neck with his own sword and severed it. Swish. Slice. Done.

"The Lord has struck him down by the hand of a woman."

The power I'd given the committee *over* me flowed *into* me.

"So I'm going to seminary anyway," I announced as I burst into rector Steve's office. "I have to study the Bible. It's a sacrament like Eucharist. Let me tell you about Judith." I was wearing a halter top and short shorts. I wanted to flirt, but he looked stern, told me to sit down. At once the portion of Judith's spirit I carried dimmed, and I was Lyn again, church reject, no longer devout, valorous, or violent.

"I told the parish what had happened, and several of them want to see the bishop on your behalf. Is that okay with you?" he said.

"Is that ever done?"

"No, but . . ."

"Are you going?" I said.

"No, but . . . better the lay folks go."

"Coward."

"I called the bishop to plead your case," he said.

"Well, good."

"I have copies of letters that people, including your parents and your younger sister Jeanie from Oklahoma, wrote to the bishop, protesting your rejection," he continued, handing me the pile of letters.

Dear Jeanie wrote for me. The youngest of the three of us Gillespie sisters, Jeanie was born with no miscarriages preceding her birth and therefore, I think, my mother's best beloved. Jeanie had married and moved far away from home, Oklahoma away. Mom never talked about it but I think Jeanie had violated one of her tenets: home is where the mother is. God knows Laurie and I had stuck close to mother/home.

Jeanie, who had stayed with the Presbyterian Church, wrote a strong letter to the bishop. Incredulous at the insult, she stated that her sister was the best and should be a priest. I loved her. I shuffled through the letters, selecting just one more to read now: the letter from my parents, composed, I knew, by Dad, because Mom would've demurred, citing her lack of formal education. The letter was eloquent. Dad's praise was pure and untinged by sarcasm—just right. (Mom might have gushed.) Dad had fallen in love with the Eucharist, the music and liturgy of the Episcopal Church, and understood my vocation. Mom was more enthusiastic about parish activities. She'd organized a Dickensian Christmas fair called Quality Street. It made money, and forty years later remains a popular annual parish event.

"Hey," I told Steve, feeling re-peppered with Judith's spirit, "why not? I'm flattered that people want to lobby for me. May be a lost cause but I adore them for trying."

Clare, a former Roman Catholic, called Diocesan House and asked for an "audience" with the bishop. He agreed. The parish patriarch, DJV, who loved football so much he'd begun to resemble one, called the shots as self-appointed coach for this scrimmage. My favorite parishioner, Francelia, in her eighties, silver-haired with wit that cut like a scythe, signed on to go. Some fifteen people from Trinity, including both sisters (Jeanie visiting from Oklahoma) and my parents, stormed Diocesan House on my behalf. Laurie remembered it this way: "We were in a big room with a very large table. Everything was ugly dark. I had never been to Diocesan House and was shocked at how dark, old, and dirty it seemed. No wonder people referred to it as the mausoleum. We sat around the table. A big armchair was at the head, obviously for the bishop. I remember waiting what seemed like a long time. I was nervous. There was very little talk as we waited. When the bishop arrived and sat down, he asked how he could help us. Ha! Maybe he thought that Steve was not properly shepherding his flock.

DJV plunged right in with his usual grace and challenged the bishop's and the committee's ridiculous dual vocation idea. For him, clearly not of the women's lib generation, this was a bold move. The bishop said nothing. Others chimed in with statements about your qualifications and sincerity—yes, even me. Jeanie was in tears most of the time and Mom tried to comfort her. As the meeting progressed we could tell it was going nowhere, but we needed to let the bishop know he was wrong and we had long memories. He was asked to reconsider, but I don't think his response was sincere. I felt unheard at the least and dismissed at the worst. It was not a pleasant experience. Looking back, I think the bishop was as scared as many of us were. I'm sure he couldn't wait to get us all out of there.

The bishop, according to follow-up grapevine reports, was hopping mad about this "irregular" confrontation. The people of Trinity, many of them with little idea of their ecclesiastical institution beyond their small home parish, found out they belonged to a church of bishops—not Catholic, but close. We Episcopalians think of ourselves as catholic without Rome—some kind of flavorful mix embracing the best of Catholicism and the best of Protestantism. We are a church in line with the historic episcopate of the Christian church, but a self-governing body, formed by two powerful streams of religious identity.

I wasn't surprised by the Episcopal rebuff but I sure as hell felt beloved in this little parish, the launching pad of my official quest for ordination, the community where I'd experienced the mercies of God. Love like this can make you as strong as rage.

I decided to take time to think—just in case I was wrong. Or God was wrong. Or Steve was wrong. Laurie, my most faithful, yet also critical supporter, added her own battery of questions to my hesitation. "Lynnie, you're an ass. Why the hell do you want to be a priest anyway?" Laurie and I had joked about just meeting each other, even though we'd known each other all our lives. We were adult women free to see each as we were rather than as our mother had interpreted each of us to the other.

"I've told you over and over. I want to celebrate the Eucharist, preach too. Why do you think it's so dumb?"

"Hasn't the damn church hurt you enough? You're a woman, for God's sake! They don't want you. You got any Pepsi?"

"But that's why they have to have me, or why I think they should. It's justice, isn't it? Women's lib. God's still with me, but I worry I'm going too fast, leaving God in the dust. Imagine!"

"You are stupider than I thought," she said. "God is supposed to lead. So be led."

"Baaa. Baaa."

"You sure as hell led *me* all these years. Okay, I don't like this follower idea, either."

"There's no place God hasn't already been anyway, right? You think I'm a bad mom?"

"What's that got to do with anything? Forget what the committee said. You're just not a little kids' mom. You don't play and do silly fun stuff like I do. Not domestic at heart, even though you can sew like a champ and bake cookies."

"I do that for love of the kids, and I made Jeanie's bridesmaids' dresses for love of her," I said. "But I'm tired of domesticity. No charge there."

"No kidding. You're having too much fun flirting around."

She was right. Flirting meant freedom more than it did sex. Laurie had done her share too. But as mothers we were different. I wasn't loving in a smoochy, aprony way, but when I planted kisses on the cheek of each sleeping child at night, I prayed they would know that my heart was breaking just trying to get its love out and into their souls.

I'd learned flirtatious ways watching my mother. One night as a teenager I'd come home early from a date and seen her perched on a man's lap, not Dad's, while he ran his unsteady hand up her thigh as she protested with glee. I'd fled to my room. Apparently, I was now catching up to my mother. Just feeling attracted to Rector Steve was enough to make me feel like a woman. Still, I longed to make a difference beyond motherhood and sexual attraction.

Calling my ravenous ambition "passion" and my unsophisticated flirting "awakening," I steadied the ship with an old favorite strategy: school. I took a semester of graduate courses in the psychology of women, counseling, group process, and social work theory at the University of Hartford and University of Connecticut School of Social Work. Part of my education was smoking pot in the back of a van in the University of Hartford parking lot with a man at least ten years my junior who had a crush on me. I declined a date, but not the pot. Pot was a bust, but the scene was worthy of a movie: sex-starved matron, thirty-nine, mother of four, worrying about cookies, manages to fend off the advances of a twenty-something while breathing deeply on her first toke and fantasizing about becoming a priest.

I loved psychology and thrived in the academic environment, but I longed to study God.

"The school of social work has established a joint degree program with Yale Divinity School," my advisor told me. "Perhaps it would suit you."

Suit me? It was a fail-safe plan. I applied to Yale and was accepted. I applied for a student loan and got it. I felt like a "man," doing business, signing agreements about money. Now I had debt. But I'd get a job. Bill didn't care as long as the debt wasn't his. He was not obstructive, but not supportive either. Then—bearing in mind Committee One's warning about "an act of defiance against church authority" and worrying that joint degree sounded like dual vocation—I wrote to the bishop about my educational plans. He replied that anyone who desired one could get a theological education. I would go to God school and forget the church.

⚑

January, 1978: Press my letter of acceptance from Yale Divinity between the pages of this year's scrapbook.

February: Persuade Bill and the kids, now 15, 13, 10, and 7, that a move closer to school, library, shopping center will make it easy to ride bikes when I can't be the chauffeur.

March 23: Have one last tearful good bye with Steve, who was leaving to go to another parish.

March 24: Bad Good Friday.

March 25: Holy Saturday and Feast of the Annunciation—Mary's big day, overshadowed by her son's death, what else is new?

March 26: Easter, the Rector's last Sunday at Trinity (lousy emotional politics), sing like a banshee in church, resurrection or no resurrection.

April: Sign my student loan application "Lyn" instead of my legal and baptismal name "Lynda."

May: Quit my newspaper job. Get elected to the parish find-a-new-rector Search Committee, chaired without discussion by DJV.

June, July: Buy a yellow vinyl-sided house close to school and town, with a big red refrigerator that John can reach. Sell North Canton house. Move.

August 1: Receive confirmation from Yale that the feds had paid my first semester's tuition. Select my courses and buy a great big heavy annotated Holy Bible. Have the car, a blue Subaru I named the Divmobile, serviced and washed.

August 7, 1978: Turn forty; thank my children, my parents, and Laurie for being surrogate parents if necessary. In my excitement, contemplate having sex with Bill but don't.

August 30: Shop for groceries and stock the refrigerator and pantry as if we'd just had a severe hurricane warning.

August 31: Give R. B. a festive eleventh birthday party.

September 1, 2, 3, 4, 5: Wash everyone's clothes. Go school shopping.

September 6, Labor Day: Bake a memorial batch of chocolate chip cookies, four dozen, freeze one; enjoy a family last-swim outing—Mom, Dad, Bev, Jill, R. B., John—complete.

Tuesday, September 7: Hop in the Divmobile and head for New Haven. Register for classes on Monday, Wednesday, and Friday, so I'll be fifty miles away from home only three days a week. Get my very own mailbox key. Listen to a welcome from the dean. Go on a walking tour of the campus. Meet a few other M-W-F commuters with whom I locate the refectory (fancy word for cafeteria at a religious institution) and bookstore. Locate the lecture hall for the next day.

Wednesday, September 8, 6 a.m.: Arc my arm over and punch the alarm clock's snooze button. Snooze. 6:15 a.m.: Get up and pad in bare feet to the kitchen to make lunches and line up the cereal array. 6:30 a.m.: Say goodbye to Bill, give and receive a hug. 6:45 a.m.: Wake up the children— the first day of school is the only day on which there are no what-to-wear traumas, no arguments about getting up so early. 7:30 a.m.: We are all ready to go our different directions; we part with kisses, good lucks, and reassurances about my love and the fully stocked refrigerator. 7:40 a.m.: Wave to the big yellow school bus as it departs. Skip back down the driveway. Kiss the Divmobile. Run into the house to get my own books. 8 a.m.: Let God know what I'm doing. Turn the key in the ignition.

Set. Breathe. Ready. Go.

CHAPTER 5 In the Beginning

"In the beginning . . ." the Old Testament professor began.

"In the beginning!" I wrote.

"In the beginning God potentiated life—over and over and over." I loved that word—*potentiated.* I'm not sure the professor said it but I heard it. I wrote it twice, white-knuckling my brand-new shiny red God-pen.

This creation story in Genesis raised the hairs on my forearms. It was a thriller, congested, overcrowded, sumptuous, exploding as it unfolded—an image of divinely ordained diversity. I listened as the professor, huge horn-rimmed glasses circling his eyes, spoke in tones worthy of worship for the beauty God's Spirit pulled from the expectant earthen matter over which it vibrated. Here I found divine sanction for gender equivalence: women and men formed in the divine image. This was not a new idea to me but I knew it in a way I'd never known it before. My whole body felt light and lit up. Everything alive was popping with power, not just the one omnipotent He-God.

The next story in Genesis, the garden of Eden myth, seemed to conflict with the grand one about creation, because now there were people in the mix—characters and a plot. But for me it was complementary. The first woman, Eve, apparently all on her own abetted by a truth-telling snake, invented sin, death, and defiance of divine will. She was a leader in sinning— pro-choice (not in the current political sense of that expression) way back then. All this with one bite from a forbidden fruit traditionally imagined to be a big, juicy, crunchy apple—Macoun, I fantasized.

"Don't miss a word in a scriptural text," the Old Testament professor boomed. "There is NO apple mentioned. We'll test you on it."

Everyone laughed. I loosened my grip on my pen. I could pass this test.

Was this the same Bible I'd read in seventh grade? I'd heard many sermons condemning Eve, and the poor snake, for the whole cosmic fall of *man,* but I marveled instead at the power this story attributed to a woman, the same power of choice given to Mary, the virgin maiden who also questioned God—this same power that religion has been trying to curse and subdue ever since. Christians called Mary good and Eve bad, but I saw two women firsts. God, annoyed at the way the Eden couple messed up a perfect project, nevertheless chose gutsy women. Someone had to keep potentiation potentiated.

Biblical study brought many scholarly things to light, all of them dazzling, yet it was the stories that fed my soul. I didn't care if they were "true," they had truth enough for me: God grappled with people as they stumbled bravely through one drama after another; not much kept them apart for long; neither gave up on the other, or on the original dynamic evolving creation. This *was* the same Bible that enlivened me as a teen.

These biblical ancients became my people, imperfect and not abandoned, choosing both hope *and* sin. I felt guilty for preferring the Old Testament to the New, but not a lot.

In my own beginning there were also two seemingly conflicting stories: finding God under the table and losing God in the theater. Was I here to resolve these beginnings? Was I here to further plumb the depths of the cookie question? This confounding collective best-selling holy biblical memoir might help me become a priest.

Managing seminary, commuting, and course work filled me to bursting with energy, but it did not improve my capacity for steadfast love. Once I told my children, "Shut up, I'm reading my Bible." I did more apologizing than ever (Sorry, I won't be home again tonight, but I promise I will . . .) and received more forgiveness (Mom, you're never here! . . .but it's okay, so then Saturday can we go . . . ?) than my children—an astonishingly resilient, bright-hearted brood—had planned on. They went on with their lives, and thank God I didn't know everything they experimented with while I was doing my own experimenting. There was good-making knowledge and evil-making knowledge for us all.

I soaked up not only biblical stories but those of all church strugglers including writings of contemporary women just beginning to find their own theological, ethical, and ascetical voices. Christian feminists called openly for gender-inclusive language, giving biblical women, often anonymous or mentioned in groups, strong voices, lobbying for full inclusion of women's ministries, writing to remind us that although Jesus was male the risen Christ was gender free. There was even a new spelling for the divine name: *Godde*—an Old English spelling with a softer more open ending than a single hard *d*.

I bumped into Joan Horwit one day in the refectory. She'd passed through the hideous bell-timed Committee One interviews with me and was the only woman to be granted postulancy. And I didn't know she was at Yale. I hadn't even thought of her, shrink-wrapped as I was in my own drama.

I asked Joan about her experience. She shared a few sparse details.

"Do you think I have a vocation to priesthood?" I asked her.

"I think you believe you do," she said, in her gravelly theater-trained voice, to the space over my right shoulder.

The spirit of paranoia had crept over us women as we tried to leap the hurdles to ordination and detect land mines along the way. We first-wavers had exchanged the politics of courage for the politics of caution. Our experience was very different from that of the women ordained "illegally," who through adversity became a community of purpose.

There was still enough leftover sweet adversity for me and my commuting buddies to overcome, like church attitudes and the family/career balancing act. We majored in lunch, argued favorite heresies, and cursed the church on whose authority we depended for ordination.

B. T. wasn't married. She had red wavy hair, not Irish or orphan Annie-kinky. Her pleasant Iowan drawl meandered. B. T. usually moved slowly, but one day she nearly knocked me down getting to the copier.

"Out of my way. I gotta get this ember to my bishop yesterday."

I jumped aside.

B. T. was mailing an ember letter, not a hot coal. Ember days on the church calendar are times set aside to pray for those entering the ordained ministry. Episcopal seminarians on the ordination track were required to write ember letters to their bishops on December 13, St. Lucy's Day, the week of Lent I, Pentecost, and September 14, Holy Cross Day. Ordaining bishops wanted to know if their seminarians were getting enlightened enough with St. Lucy, repenting enough in Lent, hot enough for the church's ministry at Pentecost, and suffering enough with our "crosses."

I lamented to B. T. "I don't even have a bishop to obey, much less write to."

"Girl, come on over for a glass of wine." B. T. lived in an apartment off campus. I dropped over.

"What's it like in Iowa?" I asked.

"Well, hot, dry, flat, and home," she said.

"What in the hell does Jesus' parable mean about it being harder for the rich to get into the divine kingdom than getting a camel through a needle's eye? I'm not rich or a camel, but I sure feel like a hulking beast in a needle's-eye church," I said.

"Well, I guess a camel transformed could get through a needle's eye," she said. "You know, I was attracted to you from the first moment I saw you."

I'd never met a lesbian before B. T. as far as I knew. I felt a stirring inside. "Let's talk about our slim chances to get ordained in the Episcopal Church. You're a woman and gay. I'm a woman and a mother. At least you're a postulant."

"You'll make it," she said.

"Forget it, B. I'm a little wispy W.A.S.P., married with children—all the right looks but . . . and if you come out, they'll never ordain you."

"Don't worry, baby, we'll make it. I love you, you know. Sure enough, fell in love with you the very first day at orientation. Let's fuck churchy talk and make love." B. T. put down her wine.

Hazy-headed, I closed my eyes and pursed my lips, mocking. She brushed my lips with hers. My eyes flew open. B. T. sat back amused. Then her lips, silken as a butterfly, sank into mine. I'd never felt kisses like this. My heart raced and my nipples swelled as my body led my mind away from itself and I fell into the tender embrace of a woman's love. I didn't know how much I'd craved that kind of soft loving until I had it.

"Better get home to the kids." I pulled away, using my safe traditional cover, a cover the church had found too "unsafe" to ordain.

B. T.'s seduction came at a time when I was feeling the urgency of love in the flesh. Was this embodied love really holy? I wasn't a lesbian. Or I was somewhere in between. My ways of being sexual were to be sexy like an adolescent whose body's in bloom but ill prepared for anything more demanding than play. Married, I could perform intercourse, but without orgasms. Having children had been an amazing bodily awakening, but not enough.

I consulted a gynecologist, who ordered me, with a wave of his imperious finger, onto the table and into the stirrups position. He then plucked a large mirror from his wall, thrust it into my hands, and instructed me to hold it above my genitals while he delivered an anatomy lecture. Behold— the sacred mystery of female sexuality shall be revealed. It was mysterious, all right—an ugly gray indiscernible mess. So? The doctor was pleased with himself, as if he'd discovered the Yukon. I thanked him for his time.

My body, the intimate exile, was restless to be reinstated. A woman friend mentioned masturbation and taught me—not by demo. My sacred little mystery had a name: clitoris. It took some fumbling, but I found mine. Contact and blast off. I understood why women sometimes cried out the divine name at such times. Where had I been?

God was on board with sex but where was the church? Sexism, I'd learned, was a symptom of underdeveloped sexuality. The church was afraid of sex, B. T. had said. So was I. My own underdeveloped sexuality had col- lided with the sexism in the church. In my seminary studies I learned that sexuality was a spiritual gift from God, not just a means to keep the race going. God dwelt in human flesh—all of it. The Bible said so. The mystics said so. Christian theology said so. Could I say so —and mean it?

Because of the old god-man's molestation, I'd fled from the full, ripe best sex could offer. Theological studies provided the context for healing my shame, especially one memorable course called "Christian Experience as Life in The Spirit." It was a journal course, packed with eager students like me looking for a course with no big tomes to read, except the sacred scriptures of their own lived experience. At first we had no idea that the "life" the course advertised was God's life and that it wasn't as transcendent as some of us figured, or hoped. The professor introduced each assignment with his own comments, and then we were to write, putting our own flesh onto the bones of abstract theological concepts like hope, holiness, grace, sin, faith, love, male and female in Christ.

"The Spirit searches everything, even the depths of God. Check First Corinthians 2:10b. Even the depths of God. Don't forget it," the professor admonished. *Even the depths of God?* Who was safe?

I got stumped trying to write on the Holy, famously defined by Rudolf Otto in his book *The Idea of the Holy* as a *mysterium tremendum et fasci- nans,* a mystery stunning enough to overwhelm and alluring enough to appeal at the same time. My mind came up with gibberish. I couldn't think.

I'm sick of mystery, sick of being a mystery. I want to know.

Pow! I was back in the theater. Words that had taken thirty-five years to form tumbled out onto blank pages—the torment of feeling trapped between desire and dread, between *yes* and *no,* between *fascinans* and *tremendum.* I wrote:

> I am about eight, sitting in a movie theater in New York City. I am between my aunt whose treat this is, and an elderly man with a shabby worn overcoat and a long white beard. I am suddenly aware that his withered hand is on my knee. He is pushing up my skirt, my brand-new dirndl skirt, my pride. It feels like ice moving up my thigh. I am beginning to freeze and sweat all at once. I wake up enough to remove his hand, but it comes back again. I am paralyzed. Then I feel a hot, dimly pleasurable sensation as his finger probes. Why don't I move? I can't. I am trapped in a net, caught between the repulsion of molestation and the attraction of clitoral sensation. I have never heard of either of these two things. They swim in upon me, nearly suffocating and drowning me in a dreadful yes/no agony of immobility. I never tell. I think something is wrong with me. It's my fault.

That night I slept the sleep of angels.

In the morning I reread what I'd written in the journal chapter called "The Organizing Power of the Holy: A Religious Experience of the Holy." I felt tenderness toward the child in the theater, so tragically small and alone. I'd thought just knowing what happened was enough, but knowledge was only the melody; when supported by the tones of my feelings and bodily sensations, the truth grew robust—and holy.

I had written the old man to death—myself to new life.

CHAPTER 6 Death Interrupts

I drove to school on a dazzling blue morning in March, 1979. When I came home at dusk the sun was gone and so was my youngest sister, Jeanie.

As I drove slowly down our driveway and parked amidst several cars I didn't recognize, Laurie ran out to meet me.

"Jeanie died," she sobbed.

Her tears soaked my shoulder after I got out of my car. I walked to the house, mystified at the scene: strange cars, people from Trinity gathered in my living room, and the new rector, Dick Simeone, sitting with his huge bandaged foot (he'd dropped an old sink in the rectory attic on his toe) propped up on a stool. I would soon learn he came on stage this way—sheer drama when he wasn't yet sure of his lines. From his seat he beckoned to me to sit down. He was the only one in the room I'd told about my fears that Jeanie might not survive this major brain surgery to remove congenital brain aneurysms. The children hovered around the edges. Bill was on his way home.

Jeanie was thirty-four and the mother of three children, a boy, eleven, and twins, nine. She'd had symptoms, like numbing and dizziness on and off through her life, and most recently two episodes of passing out. Various doctors had various theories. When X-rays showed the presence of brain aneurysms, she was directed to a neurosurgeon who said surgery should be immediate. The surgery was "successful," but Jeanie never woke up—respiratory failure was the cause of death. There had been an appointment for a second opinion, which Jeanie never kept, and which her husband Don forgot to cancel. When the reminder call came for Mrs. Steele's appointment, Don had said flatly, "She's dead."

"I don't miss her but I think of her every single day," Don told me years later, and added that his uncle, himself a neurosurgeon, eventually told him that, with her condition, Jeanie had been lucky to have her thirty-four years.

Death, like love, crashes in on life. Unlike love it makes you feel cold, dead. I drank the drink someone shoved into my hand, as if it could restore life. What did my dead sister look like? I closed my eyes, but I couldn't remember. Time fused shut. My mind set up puzzles. What was the past like with Jeanie in it? Can I live in the present without her? How can I go into the future without knowing Jeanie better, and her me?

The phone rang. My mother asked how I was. I told her "fine."

"Daddy can't come to the phone now. He's too broken up."

Knowing my father was broken up broke me up.

Later, after everyone had gone home and it was time for bed, Bill and I held each other close, a rare hospitality in these darkest days of our unraveling marriage. We'd stopped touching. When exactly had I turned my energy away from our marriage? When had I stopped trying to make things happen? When had it died? I didn't know when Bill withdrew his heart. Now my little sister was dead and I curled up like an infant on our bed. Though death creates irremediable distance between the living and the dead, it can heal distance among the living. When someone close dies, you pay attention to who is still alive. I couldn't bear another death, not now. That night Bill and I huddled into the warmth of our naked bodies. The next day we booked a flight to Oklahoma City.

Dad and Laurie and I went to pray in a local church on the day and approximate hour of Jeanie's cremation. Really we just sat there together in our separate silences. Do you know how impossible it is to imagine the whole body of someone you've loved being thrown into a fiery furnace and burned up? A crematory is a furnace that combusts at temperatures as high as 2,100 degrees Fahrenheit. It takes from seventy to two-hundred minutes, depending on the weight of the body. Jeanie's wouldn't take that long. I winced, thinking how much the fire would hurt my dead sister. Oh God. The biblical story about Daniel and his three friends being thrown into the fiery furnace for refusing to worship the emperor instead of their God popped into my mind. God showed up in the furnace and the three men emerged, as unburned as the soles of fire walkers' feet. The story was true myth—no facts but lots of truth. It helped me cry freely. Would God be there for Jeanie now? What would God look like, ablaze with flame tongues, yet unconsumed? We three sat side by side on the hard pew in the stone chapel. I didn't look to see if Daddy or Laurie was crying. I hunched up tight, put my hands between my thighs to warm them, and hoped.

Returning to Jeanie's house and seeing her husband, Don, and her three young children broke my heart. I couldn't imagine what they were feeling. I wanted to clutch them and smother them with kisses. Maybe we should have brought our children. Maybe their presence would have helped their cousins. I tried to come alive but all I felt was mute horror as I sat, alone with my thoughts, among a large gathering of people. I think we ate some of the food that the church people had prepared. My recollection is that the family stood around helplessly chatting. Maybe the ritual of to-morrow's funeral would help. I slept that night without dreams or feelings, other than a profound ache for the children.

For Jeanie's funeral, her parish church was full. People show up when a young person dies. It's like ogling a roadside accident, taking a peek at a worst fear. It's also an outpouring of impotent though authentic caring, which Jeanie's dazed husband Don would later say helped a lot and made the day both "sad and amazing."

The family crowded into a pew. I looked over at my mother, who was smiling, looking around at all the people. Where were her tears? This was her baby's funeral. As a child I used to watch for my mother's tears to tell me mine were okay, and to let me know she cared, but I never saw them.

Mom didn't cry. Had she exhausted her grief capacity on her father who died when she was twelve? Tearlessness was a sign of bravery in her generation? I decided my mother was still in shock and hoped she would share her tears with me in the months ahead. Dad just hung his head.

When Bill and I got home our children were filled with questions and joy. "Do we have to eat any more lasagna?" Lasagna remains the everlast-ing multi-meal offering at times like this. I instituted an immediate lasagna ban. "Why didn't you take us with you?" We had no good answers, no good excuses. Both of us remembered that as children we had been banished at times of death and fear, and we both remembered the terror of exile and ignorance.

"We won't ever leave you out again," Bill said.

I told them that their grandparents would bring some of Aunt Jeanie's ashes home on the plane with them and that there would be a memorial service at Trinity.

"So we all can go,'" R. B. said.

"You all can go," Bill said.

"And see the ashes?" John said.

"If you want," Bill said.

"Well, I definitely don't want to," Jill said.

John told us all about his day as he inhaled pizza.

It took some legal manipulations to get the ashes, but Dad had been determined that some of his daughter would come home with him. Jeanie's ashes would be the first to be buried in the parish memorial garden, ironically suggested and planned by me, with the help of a committee. The second set of ashes would be my father's.

"We're never leaving the kids behind again," I announced to Dick during his post-funeral pastoral visit. "How the hell old is old enough? They're sixteen, fifteen, eleven, and eight. I swear, if I ever get ordained, I'm teaching new things about the Eucharist and I'm letting people know that Jesus wept more than once. Think he made love?"

"Likely. He was human," Dick said.

"Remember the night before Jeanie's surgery when I told you about my fears that she would die?" I said. "And remember when you were leaving we almost kissed—almost?"

Dick nodded.

We sat still, listening to each other with our eyes.

"The Eucharist," I said. "It's not about understanding it. Who does? It's about love and life, not death, even though the prayers say we do it to proclaim Jesus' death. Our kids felt left out of Jeanie's funeral."

"So what about the Eucharist?"

"Kids should be included at the table. From the beginning! We had a communion over pizza and wine as we remembered Jeanie's life, not just her death. It's that simple, no?"

"You will make a very good priest," Dick said. "Have you thought of applying again for postulancy? You can, you know."

"What if I get turned down again?"

"You won't. I'll support you, and the parish will too," he said.

"I think it's too soon," I said. "What will people say if I get turned down again? And I'm not done grieving."

"People say, my ass. Most of what people say is bullshit. Just think about it," he said, and got up to leave. "Okay, pray, too, and grief lasts a long time," he added. He cocked his head to the left a little, looked at me through his thick glasses, his good eye squared off onto mine, and smiled a smile that covered his whole face, a magnet and a mirror. When he moved toward the door, he turned to face me again and reached out his hand to touch my arm. His hand was warm.

Maybe Dick was right. He could have Holy Spirit clout. After all we'd met when I was on Trinity's search committee, and now? Spooky dooky I thought. Dick had been a convert to women's ordination. His resistance had to do with his fears about loss of authority—male priests' I presumed. When I'd asked him in our search committee's interview about his views he'd launched a long sermonic rationale for women's ordination, so full of historical and theological elaborations he almost missed the point, though I caught it through his passion—and mine. The clang-clanging of our shared religious passions had felt almost erotic. That might have been the moment, if there is such a thing, when I fell in love with him—his honesty and his bullshit all together.

Dick was on my side. He was new to the diocese and overconfident but I decided to borrow his faith and apply for postulancy—again. Remembering Jeanie's indignant letter to the bishop, I mused that this could be a way to honor her. I was in my second year of seminary. Bishops change their minds with time, don't they? It had been a whole year and a half, almost two, since rejection number one.

I reapplied, and the bishop granted another screening with Committee One. I went through the whole process, including the dinging bell—all the same people as judges, the same bishop in office, and the same verdict: no. Again.

This time they judged me emotionally unstable, because I was honest in response to questions about the state of my marriage, which by then was lurching toward divorce. This time when I met with the bishop to hear his judgment he had with him an accomplice, presumably for support—for him. She was a member of Committee One who had recused herself from this second batch of interviews, because she was a member of the parish where I was doing fieldwork. That was nice of her—being there to look like my friend. I was forty minutes late for the appointment, getting lost along a way I knew by heart. When I entered the bishop's office, breathless and full of apologies, the bishop and Mrs. Splay, with her perfectly coiffed one-piece immovable orange pageboy, smiled—and smiled some more. Their pitying looks told me before they told me, and again I cried. This time I had my own Kleenex, and this time I left, eschewing their offers of comfort and without a "thank you."

I should have lied like some women did—get ordained, *then* get divorced. My lack of political sophistication, once I saw it, was mortifying, but the second rejection was humiliating to the point of despair.

No amount of loving pastoral care and attention from my colleagues, friends, therapist, or Dick took away the sting. I literally felt nauseous, boiling over with a brew of rage/fear/shame/sorrow. I reread Jeanie's letter. She believed in me. My children hovered with affection and continued to live their own lives around my consternation. I thought my mother might cry with me, but she asked me the same question I was asking everybody else. Why?

I called and wrote and interviewed everyone I could think of about what happened. One pious English cleric implied that I should know what happened. But I didn't, exactly. Laurie's standard church-as-asshole comment made the most sense, as did that of my favorite New Testament seminary professor who said with compassion, "Lyn, you don't fit the model. Look around." He was the same professor who had strenuously advised us students, "This *bath qol* in Hebrew Scripture is the voice of God. Pay attention to it, my friends. It's one of the main characters in Holy Scripture." Was this *bath qol* what I'd heard over cookies? Did it come more than once? Seeking feverishly, I went back to my class notes, grateful that I'd always been a note nerd. *Bath qol* can be translated as "the daughter of a voice"— the inner echo of a voice, soundless, soft. When prophecy faded, the rabbis knew God would not fall silent, especially in periods of decline. Jesus heard the *bath qol* calling him "son" at his baptism. I felt sure I'd heard this *bath qol* over cookies.

Oh God, let me hear your bath qol. *Please.*

The rector in my fieldwork parish suggested I talk to someone he knew who had been rejected by the church—a woman I assumed. But Elmore McKee was no woman. Elmore, small of stature and with a broad grin, welcomed me into his house, offered me a cup of tea, and then excused himself for a minute. He went into an adjoining room and I heard him say, "Are you all right, my sweetheart? Is there anything I can get for you? Let me tuck the blanket around your ankles. I'm right here. Right here."

I heard no other voice.

"Sorry to take a minute," he said when he returned. "My wife has Alzheimer's and I take care of her."

"I'm so sorry," I said, fighting the impulse to downsize my own feelings in the presence of what his must be.

"But you are here to talk about the priesthood and the church, no? You've been turned down in the ordination process. Such a cruel ordeal." Elmore shook his head.

Hearing him name it plainly loosed my own story and my grief. Elmore listened with attention. Once he interrupted saying he'd heard his wife call. I'd heard nothing and marveled that he detected a sound. I thought of the God of my childhood book who sat in the garden and listened for all "weeny" sounds. Elmore told me some of his story. He was an Episcopal priest who'd been deposed [defrocked] back in the fifties for divorce and remarriage. I was horrified, especially since I might be divorced—and marry again sometime. Elmore talked so much about the primacy of lay ministry I eventually asked him if there was a place for priests in his ministry scheme. He said, "Oh yes," in a way that told me not to probe his grief. I met with Elmore many times. He gave me hope. I knew he was a priest, no matter what the church said.

I read Jean Baker Miller's ground-breaking book, *Toward a New Psychology of Women*, published in 1976, the same year the church had voted women could be ordained, also the same year that military academies were opened to women applicants and General William Westmoreland declared about women, "We don't run the military for freaks!" I was no freak, just trapped in patriarchy. All the major institutions, even housewifery, were defined by men to keep them in power.

Miller's research consistently showed that women derived their well-being, selfhood, and maturity from mutual growth-fostering relationships, not from being an autonomous self. Women valued relationships over autonomy. Lo and behold, women weren't men. Miller's insights should have been required reading for women trying to exercise authority in the church whose traditional language described priests as "set apart." Was it that I wasn't fit or that the church's model didn't fit women? Sure I wanted autonomy, but I didn't want to be alone. How would this work as a parish priest? I'd be embedded in a community where I couldn't form close friendships? What if I fell in love? How close is close?

Women had tried to tailor their psyches to reigning models for health, written by men, for men, and about men, and gotten sick—lonely, depressed, and ashamed at their failure to attain the advertised goal of the noble and separate self. Miller had started a revolution as volcanic as Friedan's and Steinem's.

The Episcopal women who'd been irregularly ordained started a revolution, too. Women wanted power, equality, and rights—*and* the daily bread of relationships? It might become difficult for women priests to be women. Most of the ordination "rebels" did not become parish priests. The dominant parochial model, priest as lone ranger/rector, might be toxic for women. I also wondered whether the all-male potentate image of God was good for women, or anyone for that matter. All those omni- words I'd memorized in Sunday School had been conceived by men I presumed. Now, it seemed, women were not very good for God's image.

"Who ever heard of a female King, for heaven's sake?" I complained to Dick, a feminist himself who listened to all my unorthodox insights.

"I wrote to the bishop on your behalf," he said. "Don't give up."

"I know, and he never responded."

"I heard from the coadjutor bishop, though. He accused me of making *ad hominem* attacks on the diocesan bishop."

"What's *ad hominem?*"

"Too emotional, not logical," he snorted.

"Just like you," I grinned. My flamboyant hero.

But Dick couldn't explain the church, only get angry at it with me. And he couldn't answer my burning questions: why *really* had I been rejected, and why was I still in hot pursuit of a vocation the expected parameters of which I questioned?

I consulted another therapist who encouraged me to be forthright. Forthright? Emotional honesty was fast replacing feminine modesty as a sign of health and wholeness.

"Why exempt the church," the therapist said. "Shouldn't it be healthy too?

I wrote a letter to the diocesan bishop and all the members of Committee One, expressing my *forthright* anger about injustice, even made sure to speak for myself, not against them. The therapist thought it was great. The recipients did not. My anger was labeled hostile, immature, defensive, childish, and unbecoming a woman seeking ordination—anything but just plain anger or hurt. It was hard to imagine how things could be worse, but I'd made them worse.

"Now they all think they were right about me," I moaned to Dick.

"You should have done *ad hominem*," said Dick. "And for God's sake, literally, don't write to anyone apologizing."

All spiritual advice would say pray and wait. Prayer was impotent. I was looking for power, big omni-like power. The option to go congregational as B. T. had held no appeal. One of my seminary lunch buddies suggested I get a spiritual director and recommended hers. A spiritual director? Come on! Who could direct the Spirit?

The first time I met Madeleine L'Engle, a woman I already loved through her book, *A Wrinkle In Time,* I had to look up to see her face. Her six feet of height dominated without domineering. She spoke with austere authority and had a large dog named Abelard. (Peter Abelard, an eleventh-century monastic and theologian, a man of conspicuous gifts *and* sins, like fornication, held the view that Jesus Christ's life and death were to bring about moral change in humanity. Abelard's view lost favor to the interpretation of Jesus' death as ransom, atonement for the sins of humanity, a substitutionary sacrifice to get humanity back into God's good graces.) Many thought and still think that Abelard had a point. What sort of God would demand such atonement? Madeleine's dog's name clued me that she and I were Abelardians. She knew about God and knew God. She told me always to pray and expressed impatience at the church and its antiquarian attitudes about women: "Why don't these men just get on with it?"

About divorce Madeleine said there was no justification whatsoever for it, except adultery. Whose, I wondered. She didn't elaborate but gave me an assignment: find six women who had been in long-term marriages and six who had not, then interview them. I did and discovered this bottom line: all the women had considered adultery and divorce; the six who divorced said they could *not* envision themselves growing old with their spouse; the six who stayed in their marriages could. Madeleine told me to use what I'd learned and, annoyingly, didn't make a judgment either way. Like something God would do, I thought.

I asked Madeleine what she thought of the crucifix with a female corpus hanging on a cross a woman had sculpted and called the *Christa*. "It's so stunning and beautiful. It made me cry," I said.

"Well, yes, dear, it is, as a statement. But don't take it overly seriously. You're not crucified yet."

Madeleine had a way of grounding things without depriving them of their splendor. "The Spirit is the director, not me," she said, but you could have fooled me. Madeleine *was* the embodiment of Spirit Herself. I continued to see her at her home in Goshen. Her wit and her grit healed me, and set me on my feet. She encouraged me to write and pursue the studies I loved. "Go to church of course, but forget the church."

About ordination she said something I have never forgotten, a thou-shalt-not commandment, so imperious it almost told me why I'd been turned down.

"Now my dear," she said looking into my soul, "when you get ordained, and you will, do *not* become a little man."

I burst out laughing, the way a small child sometimes spontaneously does for no good reason. I had no idea exactly what this commandment might mean in its particulars, but I envisioned that T-shirt, the one about God not being a boy. How could I be a man? How could God?

I obeyed Madeleine. I was actually praying and waiting and fussing. One spring evening I sat staring down at the book I wasn't reading. I glanced at the April liturgical calendar on the wall—all white numbers, like flares for resurrection signaling the Easter season. White for new life. White for funerals and lilies. White for brides and fleshless bones. White numbers all ran together.

No one can take this away from you.

Was this the *bath qol?* I crossed a line no thicker than one hair of my head, the line from insanity to grief, from suffering to pain, from false cross to true. Oh, it hurt—and oh, it saved.

CHAPTER 7 The Old Sweater

I wore my father's sweater around for over a year after he died. Like a child, I daubed my eyes and swept dribble from the end of my nose with one sleeve of the old golf sweater Dad loved. When I lowered my arms the sleeves hung down to my knees and made me feel oversized and bulked up for a small-framed, forty-four-year-old woman in tears. I rolled up the sleeves, inhaled a whiff of Dad's smoky scent, and brushed my hand lightly over the numerous little holes—cigarette burns, maybe a moth or two—icons of the wear and tear of love.

The V neck sweater was a polyester blend, an odd mix of green and dark blue with an alligator appliquéd on the upper left. This cultural marker identified my graying-at-the-temples dad as a member of a well-mannered class of white men who played golf at country clubs and wore frightfully colorful pants to go with their monogrammed shirts and sweaters.

I loved the sweater and the man who wore it almost shabby. I wore it on and off and folded it up at night to put it in my drawer. I patted it, tongue-tested any damp spots for saltiness, and murmured, "What's the point?" Dad used to say *what's the point?* a lot. I never knew exactly what he meant. I got a clue once when, to my astonishment, Dad signed up for an assertiveness training course I'd offered in the parish and talked about how hard it was for him to speak up for himself. He'd have to confront the house painter about a sloppy job and get stomach cramps, then never ask for what he wanted, and then, I knew, though he didn't say, have a drink. It gave *me* stomach cramps to witness his vulnerability. At the same time I felt from him a humble praise as he let me be his teacher. I desperately proffered silly assertiveness do's and don'ts when what I'd wanted to do was give him my heart.

What *was* the point? I resolved not to wear the sweater the next day— until the next day.

Dad died of esophageal cancer in 1983, not long after the church had turned me down a second time and a month before my divorce would be final. His death brought an abrupt and painful end to his seventy-one years—too few, for the length of my love.

My father loved his gin martinis, his whiskey manhattans and, after pancreatitis and four years of abstinence, his dry-as-you-can-get-it sherry. His practice had an aesthetic and a ritual. Each drink had its own hue: white, dark amber rose, and pale yellow; each had its own vessel and adornments—green olives pierced by red toothpicks for the one in the long-stemmed triangular glass, orange peels and bright maraschino cherries for the one in the stout squat tumbler, and the zest of a lemon twist for the one in the six-inch-tall, thick-rimmed glass with the sailboat on it.

When Dad drank, smoke from his Lucky Strikes and later their "safer" filtered heirs, Herbert Tareytons, curled around his head, creating a mystical aura. Alcohol and cigarettes soothed his mood as nightly they massaged his lips, throat, and lungs with toxins, the puffs and sips of which gave him undeniably beautiful smiles and sighs of deep peace. He was in a heaven of his own. No one, not even my mother, got through his pearly gates.

I didn't know which of his beloved friends killed him; nor did I blame him for his ignorance or his death. I just remembered how inadequate I used to feel, my heart stretched thin with longing, when I noticed how his chosen companions could fill in the blanks in his life and make him happy—as good soul mates do.

Dad developed reflux symptoms in early July, underwent surgery in late July, and on January 2nd, he died. His brief illness intersected my ordination grief, and my mid-life struggle to find my own identity—or at least my own brand names, politics, and religious beliefs separate from my parents' hard-earned, post-Depression, suburban, Republican, alligator-adorned lives.

The second day of January was icy cold that year. My mother called at 6 a.m. with the announcement that Daddy had died. I slid back under the covers in my queen-size bed, whispered the news to no one, and closed my eyes.

Dad was gone.

I lay still and remembered our life together.

Dad's last name, and mine before marriage, was Gillespie. When as an adult I visited Scotland, I knew immediately it was mine—bleak hillsides blanketed with heather, sharp cliffs, raging seas, Celtic isles—austere beauty, right to the point. I found out the name Gillespie means "son of a bishop" and the clan under which Gillespie was listed is MacPherson, which means "son of a parson."

When Dad was afraid on my behalf he'd call me Lynda. Like the night he'd caught me running across our lawn after midnight, sneaking out to meet Bill, and bellowed "LYNDA" from the front door with such force, I sped back. Secretly relieved at being apprehended—which at fifteen was less scary than teenage sex—I slithered by him and went up to bed. No more was said. That my father had called me my full name, unsweetened by a nickname and full of power because he'd given it to me, was enough for me to know he loved me. Or when Dad argued with me I'd become Lynda. Like when we drank together and waged mighty political warfare over our different "alligators." When I changed my political party affiliation I'd felt like a "Judas" sneaking into the town hall to accomplish a dirty deed. To Dad I was Lynda, a Democrat with a platform, a feminist, a Jesus fan full of rant about the poor, and a daughter who sparred politics and got her nerve from strong drink just like her dad.

My father's reserve had commanded respect. But as a child all I wanted was to jump into his lap as he sat in his appointed chair.

"Hi, Daddy," I'd say as I stood before him.

Silence.

"I had a bath." Though a powerful surge of energy flooded my small four-year-old body, I couldn't jump into his lap because the triangular glass was in the way.

No less naive or full of longing at age twenty-one than I was at four, I'd called him from college. "Hi, Dad, I just got elected to Phi Beta Kappa."

"There must be some mistake." He laughed then added, "Just kidding. That's great."

Brimming with success at forty-three, I'd scarcely noticed when my father announced to the assembled guests at my graduation party: "We're not sure how this happened but Lynnie has just graduated from Yale Divinity School." Everyone knew he was just kidding. So did I, laughing along with the crowd.

When I'd told Dad of my aspirations to be a priest he'd asked why, a variation on the theme of "What's the point?" When I told him I wanted to celebrate the Eucharist, he didn't say a thing but looked at me—no kidding, no judgment, no cocktail in the way. I started to babble. "You don't need to explain, Lynda," he smiled. "I get the point."

Dad loved the Episcopal liturgy. At his confirmation I'd watched him go forward and kneel in front of the bishop who laid his hands on Dad's head and prayed: *Strengthen, O Lord, your servant, McDonald, with your Holy Spirit; empower him for your service; and sustain him all the days of his life.* The whole congregation said aloud "Amen." I remember feeling proud enough to applaud, happier than I'd felt when he'd altered his drinking habits to keep pancreatic pain at bay. But this confirmation decision was freely his own. Dad had a religious turn of heart like I did. It had brought us closer. He had written the elegant letter on my behalf to the bishop (the same bishop who had confirmed him, and rejected me.) That letter had done nothing for the bishop but everything for me.

When I'd told Dad that Bill and I were separating and might get divorced, his eyes were clear but moist. Again I'd tried to explain myself, and again he'd stopped me. He knew me better than I thought; he knew me before I knew me.

What was my father's dying really like? I forced myself back to remember him at the hospital. Sights and sounds of the intensive care unit flooded my mind: loud rhythmic whooshes, gurgles, thumps and beeps, the internal workings of a human body from the outside in. Dad—ghastly and ghostly—laid on the propped-up bed, oxygen clips in his nose, intravenous lines running all over his upper body like interlaced freeways, a big bandage covering a hole in the side of his neck, his eyes bulging with terror and longing. And the surgeon telling us he "got it all"; then Mom commenting how good Daddy looked. Seeing her husband of almost fifty years in this moribund state made her stand up very straight and burnish her positive affect to a high gloss.

The cancerous esophageal tumor was gone, but so was the passageway for food and drink. Mere nutrition, a pale substitute for the joy of taste and chew and swallow, came through a feeding tube inserted from outside. Dad couldn't eat or drink. Saliva drained through another tube in the side of his neck. His customary silence had become melancholic, broken by curses at his incontinence, by impatience at my mother's distaste and ineptitude with the basics of nursing, or by smiles at his grandchildren.

The surgeon had told us that a surgical reconnection between his stunted esophagus and his stomach might be possible. He might eat—and drink. For days, wild-eyed and wordless with concentration, he spit out his saliva, using box after tiny box of hospital tissues.

"Dad, what's going on? Is there pain? Why are you catching all your saliva? You have a bag to do that for you."

"Can't," he said, shaking his head.

"Can't what?"

"Swallow. Might jeopardize the chances for the reconnect."

"Dad. No. That's wrong. I listened carefully to the surgeon. You can swallow all you want. That's what the bag is for. It has nothing to do with the reconnect."

He smiled, closed his eyes, and swallowed—twice. So did I.

It took four months for my father to realize the likely truth.

"There won't be a surgical reconnect, Frank," he'd told his former housebuilder and friend, the first person to hear my father say the truth out loud—a mere acquaintance who wouldn't cry or try to persuade him otherwise.

We, all but my mother, had guessed this and waited for my father to acknowledge it. I don't know how he convinced my mother to stop pretending. It was November; our spirits fell with the leaves.

At Christmas, my father was almost jolly as he sat at the head of the family dining room table in his wheelchair and ordered black, strong, hot coffee.

"You can't eat right. How will you have coffee, Big G?" asked twelve-year-old Sam, Laurie's son.

"Haven't I told you I can make things work?"

"You fixed broken toys and cars, but . . ."

"No buts . . ." said my father, with a wink.

The children, my four and Laurie's three, ranging in age from nineteen to twelve, had gathered around his wheelchair to watch the nurse Maggie set up additional tubing and a bowl to catch the coffee. Dad took a big sip, rolled his eyes in wonder and smacked his lips. The coffee, much of it spilling from the loose tube connection, ran down and out—fast.

"Did you get any, Big G?"

"You bet I did, and boy did it taste great." My father laughed, sucked the last bit of life out of his cigarette, and reached to touch the boy's arm. I thought for a second he would take him into his lap.

"Merry Christmas everyone." He raised his coffee cup and, without drinking, toasted Christmas.

The day after Christmas Dad went to bed to die, choosing, it seemed to me, not to live this way. It took him a week and he did not go gently into that good night. My mother, Laurie, and I kept vigil.

I felt grateful for Dick, whose mother had recently died and whose father had died in a plane crash when Dick was in college. He listened and talked about death and God and parents. As Trinity's priest he had ministered well to my parents while trying to be their pastor and my lover at the same time. Yes, my efforts to stay away from Dick and hang onto my moral axis for the sake of the church had failed.

My father could be cruel when he felt helpless. One evening he shouted: "Peggy, where the hell are my bed pads? Goddamn stupid broad." My mother's face crumpled. She turned and fled. It wasn't the first time I'd seen my father ridicule her. Mom had her way of ridicule too. She once told us she'd laughed when my father had confessed an affair early on in their marriage. I didn't know who to feel sorrier for, him or her.

One day Dad raised his head and upper body from his death pillow and, with a piercing look and hoarse voice, asked me, "What's the point?" Then his head flopped back, and his heavy mass of black-and-white hair splayed onto the pillow. It was a question I couldn't answer, so I said: "I don't know, but if you find out, Dad, let me know."

The night before he died was my watch. Lying on a sofa outside his room I'd let the chimes of the grandfather clock measure the frequency of my father's groans—heralds of death that mocked traditional images of a soul's winged ascent. To where? I came to detest the sound of grandfather clocks. Tick tock, gong, gong. The clock tolled on; my father moaned out his salvation, and I sank into an uneasy sleep.

The last time I saw my father he was dead. His body was limp, his head bobbed and dangled, along with his scrawny bare legs, over the arms of the burly funeral director who—without ceremony—carried my dead father out of the house to the waiting hearse. How, on those spindly stick-figure legs, did Dad ever play golf?

It was Sunday. I went to church and in silence absorbed the community's presence. By rote, I walked to the communion rail to eat Christ's body and drink Christ's blood, glad for Dick's steady hands pressing the bread into mine with a gentle squeeze. Many things would have to happen soon— like telling and comforting my children, and telling Bill, who had loved my father like a father, his own having died of alcoholism. But for now, sit in church, feel the hard wooden scoop of pew beneath me, taste the tasteless food. What *is* the point?

Between the morning of Dad's death and that afternoon, I returned to my parent's house. My mother had stripped his sick room of all its accouterments.

"Where's all Daddy's stuff? I asked.

"Gone. Out of here. I hated all that ugly medical equipment," she said, and turned her back. "Now the room is as it should be."

The bed my father had died in was neatly made, the green-and-blue floral spread drawn up and the pillow in its matching slip. I knew by tomorrow my mother's bed would be back in its rightful place next to his, with the small mahogany bedside table in between. I would at that moment have been grateful to spot his bedpan. But there was nothing.

"Mom. Damn it. At least can I have the red sweat suit he wore at the end?"

"I gave it to Maggie. Look around for something else," she said, turning to leave, but not before she turned her stiffened face in my direction. I thought I saw tears glued onto it. She was gone before I could embrace her.

I closed the door and leaned against its solidity before I moved to rummage through Daddy's closet and drawers. I found his old golf sweater.

Dad's funeral was at Trinity. His ashes, in their cardboard container, were veiled and stood on a small stand in front of the altar. When the ground softened to receive them, they would go into the earth in the memorial garden right next to his youngest daughter's. Ashes—gray, fine, but mingled with chunks of bone—were all that was left. The reduction fascinated the young boy grandchildren. Dick preached with affection, ending his homily with *arrivederci*, not knowing a single other Italian word but that, and no one but him Italian. Brilliant. He'd loved my dad.

After the funeral and the post-funeral eat-drink-and-remember gathering, Dick and I wanted to be together in the inevitable way. Dick was by this time divorced, and I was on the way to it, but the technicalities of commandments were not anywhere near our hearts. We fell greedily, wordlessly, into each other's arms.

I grieved, puzzling over the mysteries of God, the mystery of my father, and the mystery of the church. In Frederick Buechner's book, *Whistling in The Dark: A Doubter's Dictionary*, he honors tears and advises us to pay close attention to them and where they lead. I agree. When I let my tears flow I usually learn something from my heart. I followed my tears.

I kept wearing the sweater, unsure why. Finally I threw it away—reverently but, yes, into a waste basket.

CHAPTER 8 Smitten

I'd fallen in love with foolish abandon more than a few times in my life, but now I was falling in love with a machine, an adorably plump burnt-umber Crock-Pot, my live-in cook. A friend had suggested this new invention to me, saying it might ease my panic over cooking.

"You've never cooked, Lyn," she said. "So why do you think you have to aspire to gourmet cooking for two teenage sons who eat junk—and in a small galley kitchen to boot? It's irrational."

"I know, "I said, "but I've gotta prove I can be a little domestic."

"Lyn," said my dear budding-feminist friend, "Geraldine Ferraro ran on a presidential ticket. Women are moving out."

"Ferraro lost," I said.

"So you have to turn into a cook?" she said. "You should be worried about money, loneliness, remarriage, or insanity. At least you got the damn Crock-Pot."

We hung up, her in loving disgust and me left staring at my Crock-Pot. It provided two things I'd failed at: fidelity and home cooking. I hadn't told my friend that; nor had I mentioned that my near-veneration of the Crock-Pot was a safer obsession than the church and wanting to be a priest while falling in love with a priest.

Bill and I were separated, and I'd moved into a small condominium with R. B. and John. Bev and Jill were in college. I was working as a chaplain at Hartford Hospital, but that job was a two-year internship. Everything terrified me—making money, wearing a beeper, being a divorced woman alone, my emergent feelings for Dick Simeone, dwelling still in the shadows of shame—except this magic Crock-Pot. I would come home after a long day, and there on the counter stood my "savior," its glass top covered with sweet sweat, its belly full of a hot meal, one of four: chicken smothered in chicken noodle soup, pork chops smothered in tomato soup, stew smothered in its own juices, enhanced by ketchup and canned gravy, or pot roast smothered in cream of mushroom soup. My Crock-Pot became an icon of the peace that passes all understanding the Bible promises. I learned to simmer, and as I simmered, I wrote poems, like this one I called Priest's Song. (It was later published in *Women's Uncommon Prayers.*)

> When I have no title I make
> one up—irreverend.
> When I have no collar I roll
> my neck round.
> When I have no church I steeple
> my fingers.
> When I have no pulpit I preach
> running.
> When I have no altar I celebrate
> my back yard.
> When I have no bloody wine I shed
> tears.
> When I have no bread I am
> a sacrament.
> When I have no God I pray
> anyway.

As I simmered I dreamt up anxiety situations. One felt nearly prophetic.

> *I'm sitting on the back stoop of the farmhouse. I stretch out my toes to bake. My toes tap little pebbles in the path ahead of the stoop. I reach down for them. I pick up five. I stroke them, finger them, smile, twist them around and flirt with them because I'm eleven and everything is beginning to look sexy to me. I turn around and scowl at the screen door which I have just slam-banged, its clatter exciting— an annunciation of me. My mother yells. "Stay out there, Lynnie. Damn, I told you not to slam that door." Suddenly, I am David, a boy in a Bible story who volunteered to slay a huge giant named Goliath with only a slingshot and five smooth stones. I put my five pebbles in the front pocket of my jeans. I sit, sniff freshly mown hay, stare out at acres of corn slow-dancing with the breeze. I frown, pat my pebble pocket, then get up and walk back into the kitchen. I bang the door but with only half my strength this time. No one is in the kitchen. I open the cabinet, take down the large peanut butter tin, get two slices*

of white bread from the loaf in the bread box, slather both slices thick
with peanut butter—no jelly—and smack them together. They stick.

I leave two pebbles on the counter near my mother's half-empty
coffee mug with the bright red half-moon of lipstick on its rim. I take
my sandwich and leave by the screen door. It bangs on its own—an
annunciation of itself. I walk to the edge of the corn field with my
peanut butter sandwich and my three leftover pebbles and head off.
I walk down the golden aisles of corn and disappear. You can't even
see the top of my head.

All at once my stoop is back and I sit down on it. Now I am
forty-five. Still in jeans with pebbles in my pocket. There is no house
or screen door. I stand up straight. I am David again. I stretch out
my arms and make an altar of the falling apart picnic table which
time and decay have spared—somehow, somewhat.

I rise from the stoop and walk away, out through the waving,
whispering corn. You can see my head above the corn.

As I simmered I also dreamed myself awake with thoughts of everything that has to do with erotic love—and Dick. He was not like any priests
I'd met, and my relationship with him, though illicit, didn't *feel* superficial,
or sinful.

Trying to save my already snapped marriage *had* felt superficial. Divorce had been a ghost in our house for ten years. Bill had said he would
live this way, but I could no longer bear the haunt or the charade. And, in
case I ever applied *again* for ordination, I needed evidence of my sincere
efforts to preserve marital bliss.

"We have to try family counseling," I said.

"What's that?" Bill asked.

"We all go to see a counselor together," I said.

"All of us?" Bill said.

"Yes, I've seen it work on stage. This famous family counselor, Carl
Whitaker, assembled a whole family, including aunts, cousins, a grandpar-
ent or two. Whitaker watched them interact, commented, and made sug-
gestions. We should try it."

"Well, I'm not going on stage," Bill said, and started to walk away.
"We're fine. I just need to stay home more."

"Yeah, like that lasts? I'm calling."

"The kids will hate this," he said.

We sat stiffly; Bev, sixteen, slouched; Jill, fifteen, held her father in her
glare; R. B., just a teen and calling himself Rob, looked around for a chance

smile or a chance to smile; John sat erect on the edge of his chair; and Bill kept his arms crossed over his chest, fists tucked under each arm. I sat alone on a small ironic love seat.

To break this stalemate, the counselor suggested Bill and Jill exchange compliments. They looked at each other. We waited. Finally Bill said, "She's pretty." Jill said, "He's handsome." They moved on to "intelligent," then "nice" when the counselor interrupted and suggested we try family sculpture, a nonverbal way to make a picture of the family dynamic. That might be easier, he said. Each of us in turn positioned the others inside an imaginary family circle according to how the "sculptor" perceived where we stood in relation to one another. All of us except Rob had created pretty much the same arrangement: Bev, Rob, John, and Mom clustered together, Jill a bit distant with one foot in the imaginary circle and one foot outside it, and Bill outside the circle altogether. Then it was Rob's turn. He took his task seriously, placing Bill in the center of the circle, me next to Bill, and the four children closely gathered around us. Pleased, he looked to the counselor who said in a voice soft enough that he could have been speaking to Rob alone, "Is this the way it is, or the way you wish it were?" Sorrow settled over us. I knew I would be the one to have to pronounce our marriage dead.

When we assembled our children to tell them, Bill stood with his arms crossed over his chest, his mouth drawn tight, and said, "Your mother's leaving me." Then he turned and walked away. I don't remember what happened next, except I wondered if the children already knew what we adults hadn't dared to know out loud. Later Rob told me he was sure this family meeting was called to confront something he'd done wrong. This should have given me pause, but I was preoccupied about being the designated sole culprit and the one to initiate divorce. To the members of a family, divorce feels like every joint in the body dislocates at once, and the body will never be reassembled in the same way again.

In February 1983, I stood alone in the little box next to the judge's bench, answering the attorney's simple questions. "Is your name Lynda Hall Gillespie Brakeman?" He and I had agreed that I would answer only yes-and-no data questions. This wasn't a trial, though I still felt this divorce was more my fault than Bill's because I had made the decision he refused to make, and because after all I was an adulterous woman. The law called our divorce no-fault.

My attorney and I had done an autopsy on almost every aspect of the marriage, except the bonding and rending power alcohol had exerted on our relationship over the years. It was a dark chapter. I'd denied the extent of Bill's drinking and my own and wasn't aware of the familial addictive patterns in which I was embedded. I recognized how I'd tried to become an alcoholic to stay married (following Bill's suggestion that the couple who drinks together stays together) and then enjoyed it all by myself: once a hangover had forced me to break a promise I'd made to John to take him with his young girlfriend to the beach for the day; instead I went home and threw up.

The attorney dealt in cold, hard facts, not neurotic ones. He pressured me to ask for more in child support payments, which Bill could deduct when he filed to pay income tax. I wanted to take the payments in alimony, income on which I, not Bill, would pay taxes. It was, I told my attorney, my small way of contributing to our children's college educations. It was, he told me, foolish, given my limited earning powers compared to Bill's. It was, I said, my decision as the plaintiff.

The air in the courtroom hung stale. Steam radiators hissed as if voicing all the unfought fights, the unfelt passions, the unspoken words of love that nested in the hearts of wives and husbands who were now plaintiffs and defendants. Yet the faces of the soon-to-be-uncoupled couples were bland. The steady hum of lawyerly work, papers spilling out of briefcases, gave me an uncanny feeling of emotional safety and kept my eyes and skin dry.

I remember feeling very far away from God until I noticed that the courtroom looked like a church—uncomfortable wooden benches like pews, several levels of architectural hierarchy. Observers sat like worshipers at floor level. Attorneys with their clients sat, bride's side and groom's side, one step up from the floor where choir and clergy usually sit in churches. The witness stand was raised on a platform like a pulpit. And the judge's stand was higher still, like a celebrant's place at a high altar. A gate separated the judge's stand and witness box from everything else, just like the altar rail in many churches, which separates the liturgical party and, architecturally at least, God, from communicants as they receive their bread and wine. The architecture might fit for the purposes of a court of law, but for a Church of Love? No wonder people still thought God was a distant and exacting judge—male. Priests aren't meant to pass sentence, only bread. If I were ever ordained I would try to make changes. When that altar rail gate is closed, even secured with a bolt, I shudder.

BANG. The judge's gavel pulled me back to the courtroom. Mrs. Brakeman and Mr. Brakeman had given mutual consents, just as we had twenty years ago at our marriage. No objections. The settlement was in order, and Mr. Brakeman withdrew his motion to contend. I hadn't known there was such a motion, but instantly it all made sense: dead trust, dead marriage. We were pronounced divorced—"single and unmarried"—as simply as we'd been pronounced "man and wife" according to the 1928 Book of Common Prayer. Both decrees were made from on high, one accompanied by a smile, the other by the sharp report of a gavel. The marriage had been sacramentally indelible, secured by God and therefore indissoluble except by God, or so it was written. The divorce? Was it too a sacrament, an outer sign of an inner invisible grace? For better or worse, I didn't know.

No longer a couple, Bill and I left. What is the right gesture at such a moment—kiss goodbye at the courthouse door? Shake hands? I remember walking out into the cold midwinter streets of Hartford and staring blankly, trying to remember where I'd parked the car.

⚘

"I still want to be a priest," I told Carol, my next therapist.

"What?" she said. "You don't think they'd ordain a divorcée *and* an adulterous woman, do you? Lyn, that's nuts."

"Jesus forgave one," I said.

Carol broke into buoyant laughter. She couldn't stop. I joined in at first, but then started to feel huffy. "It's not *that* funny." I said.

"I'm sorry," she said, but she couldn't stop. "I just can't help it. It's not you."

"The hell it's not, Carol. I'm outta here," I said, grabbing my bag and leaving without paying.

When I returned the next week Carol was still there. "About time you got angry," she said. "But seriously, Lyn. Your passion is so real. Pursue your dream, powerful woman. I'm for you."

"I feel powerful," I said.

"How powerful?" she asked.

"Bull powerful," I said.

"Be the bull," Carol said.

"Now who's nuts?" I said, but Carol didn't laugh.

"Well, if you're not going to be the bull, this session is over," she said as she rose from her chair of power and went over to her desk to do paper work. I sat alone facing an empty chair, nursing venomous thoughts about Carol, who was playing matador tricks. I reached for my purse to write out a check for the half-over session when out came the bull. I still can't believe this happened, but I began to paw the floor, snort, and make roaring sounds. I was being the bull, a raging, charging, ferocious bull—no Ferdinand with a flower. When my anger subsided I looked up and saw Carol again for the first time. She was beautiful, and I'd never noticed.

"Are there words?" Carol asked.

I sang part of a hymn, a warlike hymn about how humans, referred to as "men," were waging wars and "building proud towers that would not reach to heaven." The refrain after every violent verse was, "Thy kingdom come, oh Lord, thy will be done."

I made no attempt to analyze this experience, but I knew how angry I was. And oddly, my anger planted me more firmly than ever in my voice as a woman, while at the same time confirming my desire to be a priest in the church of God—the same God who'd first listened to me under a table and years later asked me such a strange question in my kitchen.

The church, despite my problems with it, and its with me, was capable of doing the best imitation of the holy I'd ever encountered, and it was all in the name of Christ. If I wanted to be a sacramental priest, I'd better get to know Jesus better.

"You need a Jesuit for Jesus," said a Roman Catholic chaplain colleague.

"Where do I find a Jesuit?" I asked.

"On a directed retreat," she told me with excitement in her voice.

"What's that?" I said.

"Silence and prayer. You'll be amazed. When you pray with biblical Scripture you'll meet Jesus." Prayer okay. Silence not okay.

I met Pierre Wolff, my first Jesuit, at Mercy Center, a Roman Catholic retreat center in Madison, Connecticut. It was the eighties, a decade when everything of moment in my life conspired to tumble together and happen at once. I'd never heard of a silent directed retreat but trusted the zeal of my Catholic friend and signed up for a weekend. Some thirty or so retreatants, mostly women, mostly sisters, and me, assembled on the first night. I sat with my journal in my lap—ready to meet Jesus, ready to take notes. The murmurs of small talk stopped when a small man briskly entered the room, followed by three Mercy sisters—nuns who looked like ordinary women. Pierre, a small dark-haired man with a cleft nose, two bulbs of unequal size at its tip, wasn't exactly handsome, but he had a gruff, impatient charisma that seemed important. At introductions we all said our names and where we were from; Pierre said in his thick accent, "I am Pierre from France." Except for one twenty-minute meeting each day with our director, we were to be silent—even at meals. I could manage that for just a weekend. The only clear instruction, besides silence, was that when we went to see Pierre we were not to inquire how he was. "I am fine, and you are fine. Just get on with the business of what is happening in your prayer time." He waved his hand dismissively and departed as suddenly as he'd come in. I hoped one of the three sisters would be my director, but Pierre was my assigned director.

That night I fretted about my Jesus ignorance. I'd heard of him of course in Sunday School, and studied the New Testament and Christian theology. I knew *about* Jesus. But what was he like? Another man-God? Not as obtrusive as Pierre I hoped. After Dad died and Mom downsized, I'd found a church bulletin she'd saved. It was dated December 24, 1946, and on it in pencil, I'd written in tiny well-executed letters: *Where did he come from?* It was the obvious Christmas question for a curious child, but now I wondered if there was a connection between my Jesus interest and my desire to be ordained.

Pierre established the following:

- that it was my first retreat

- that I wanted to meet Jesus

- that I had four children he knew were perfect (in other words, don't waste time telling him about them)

- that I wanted to be an Episcopal priest, but was having trouble getting ordained.

Then he said, "Pffft. We see about Jesus, yes? St. Ignatius shows the way: you read a Scripture story or psalm or passage slowly, then you close your eyes, and wait to see what happens, what God might be showing you. Oh, you can say a little prayer for guidance (which he pronounced *guee-dahnce*) or grace if you like. After the prayer experience, write your feelings in your *journelle*. Start with Psalm 139. Questions?"

"But Jesus isn't in Psalm 139," I said.

"Jesus is in everything," he said, and waved me off.

I read the psalm, closed my eyes, and waited. Nothing. I went for a walk around the spacious grounds and on the beach along the sound. I tried the psalm again that evening and read:

O Lord, you have searched me and known me.
Even before a word is on my tongue,
O Lord, you know it completely. . . .
You hem me in, behind and before,
and lay your hand upon me. . . .

Hemmed in? I slammed the Bible shut. I didn't have to close my eyes and wait for God. I knew right away this was not my psalm, not the God I'd met under the table, nor the Jesus I'd hoped for. I wrote that down. Pierre was impressed by my strong reaction and thought it might be spiritual. "Stay with it, Lyn, and this psalm you hate will unfold. But not right now. Now you read Mark chapter number ten, verses thirteen through sixteen. Then imagine the scene, put yourself into it, and see what Jesus is like."

The ancient scene appeared like this before my inner eye.

Crowds of people, noisy, jockeying for position. Parents shoving their own children forward and the disciples pushing them back. I see Jesus angry, his eyes flashing, his voice raised, his arms motioning disciples and parents aside and beckoning the children to come nearer. I am about four, dressed in a red pinafore and red party shoes, my dark hair parted in the middle with bows to secure it. I stand back, frowning and sucking my thumb. Then, like in a dream, I am right in front of Jesus with my thumb and my frown. I feel his touch on my head. It is warm, light. My thumb drops from my mouth. I look up. And then, just as quickly as it had appeared, the scene fades and Jesus is gone.

"So, did you like Jesus, now that you met him?" Pierre asked on Sunday.

"Yes, I liked him a lot. Do you think what I got was a blessing?"

"Well, it wasn't a rejection, was it?" Pierre chuckled.

After that I wanted more of this kind of direct connection. I kept praying this way and went on more retreats at Mercy Center, some for a week at a time. I returned to Psalm 139 with caution. Over and over I prayed it until slowly the intimacy of God's presence came through to me, closing any distance that might have kept me from knowing how well God desired to know me. I had confused the "hemming in" God of the psalmist's prayer with my mother's brand of intimacy which had felt more like control than love. I softened into sadness thinking about me and my mother—how hard she'd tried to get to know me, even once reading my diary and telling me she had done it to get to know me better, and how equally hard I'd resisted her advances. God's way of knowing felt just as persistent but not as invasive. The psalm I'd first hated helped me feel compassion for Mom and myself, and with it came assurance that God was neither mother nor father, as traditional metaphors would have us think. These were images for children, and I was growing up. The biblical Word was much greater than its words. A crusty Jesuit from France and his beloved mentor from Loyola were helping me become a woman.

Pierre told me that all the Scriptures of my life were in the Bible somewhere. "You will find a story to pray with that offers you perfect praise, like the little one experienced under the table," he said.

I sought and found my praise story in the Gospel according to Mark, chapter fourteen:

> An unknown woman enters a room full of men who are making big political plans for a triumphal entry into Jerusalem where Jesus/ Messiah would take over, they thought. The woman has another idea. She enters the room full of men, walks up to Jesus, reclined at the table, with her jar of nard and pours it over his head, anointing him before death. Scandal. The men grumble and rebuke her, but Jesus defends her gesture as "beautiful" and prophesies that what she has done will be told in memory of her whenever the gospel is proclaimed the world over.

Jesus and this woman saw beneath surface reality. I loved this story and abandoned my heart to it. It contained the feelings of a lifetime and portrayed Jesus in solidarity with a woman. I let the Spirit and what Pierre called my *beeg* spiritual imagination place myself into the ancient scene which unfolded this way:

> *I walk into a room full of men. I feel scared, but I keep going till I reach Jesus. I look down at him, right into his eyes. He stands to face me and waits. I open my jar of nard and, unexpectedly, I throw it all over him with words of rage and sorrow. He just stands there, precious perfume dripping down all over his face. The men in the room go into an uproar about this affront and the wasted ointment, but Jesus shuts them up, and says to me: "Thank you."*

This story in Mark and Matthew contains no implication that the anointing woman is somehow less than. A similar story written later in Luke presents the woman as a groveling sinner. In John she is demoted to a posture of submission, identified as Mary of Bethany, crouching to anoint Jesus' feet with her tears and wipe them with her hair. The later accounts I knew were written at a time when the young Christian church was inching toward institutionalization and entrenched patriarchal politics. These politics remain entrenched centuries later. Woman as humble servant? Not for me. I needed the woman in Mark who stood up. This story as I prayed with it helped heal much of my anger at men; it gave me that mattering feeling I'd known under the table, and courage to keep on fighting to get ordained. Jesus did not judge my anger. Mark's Jesus in fact affirmed the woman and bestowed upon her a "eucharist," a remembrance of her bold anointing gesture. He might as well have ordained her, and me, on the spot. I'd hang onto her spunk. I would buy that T-shirt.

🏃

"Out in public?" I looked at Dick as if he were crazy.

"We can't hide forever. Our divorces are final now. Come on. It's a symphony concert, for godssake. We'll be lost among crowds. Besides, it's André Watt," he said.

"Technically we're not adulterers, but I may try again for ordination. There's a new bishop now," I said. "Wouldn't it be better to play it safe?" Then after some thought, I asked, "How come the church didn't come after you while you were still married?"

"They pretended they didn't know and technically they only had hearsay and rumor about us. Or maybe they like us," he grinned. "And maybe they're all doing the same thing."

"And just maybe it's because you're a man. You don't see any men being hauled before Jesus for adultery, do you? Just one lone woman to be stoned."

"Jesus went against the rules of his day and forgave her," Dick said.

"Jesus forgave her, and I bet that when he bent down to write on the sand where only she could see, he wrote, 'Where's the guy?' But okay, the symphony."

The symphony was our first public date. We were both divorced by now and shouldn't have been worried. But you only function with half a brain when you're in the habit of hiding and wondering just how notorious a sinner you might be. Our post-divorce dating made pre-divorce rumors hard to deny. Besides, our pre-divorce relationship had been exposed, thanks to a barroom conversation between Bill and the husband of Dick's warden. The husband told the warden and the warden told the bishop. The "news" had landed on the desk of the Rt. Rev. Arthur E. Walmsley, not long after he was consecrated as bishop of Connecticut in 1981. One of his priests, Dick Simeone, was carrying on with a parishioner, me—*extra*maritally. Arthur, the bishop who had distaste for *ad hominem* attacks on authority, delegated the nasty investigative task to his bishop suffragan. Dick and I were summoned separately. The suffragan asked about our unsavory past, which we both denied, then told us each that if Christ was in our relationship it would bear good fruit. We both scoffed at this Christian jargon. We were spared further judgment. So maybe it wasn't empty jargon.

"In Christ" was the way the bishop who had rejected me had signed the letter he wrote to me showing no objection to my going to seminary. And Arthur Walmsley, when he had been Bishop Coadjutor, automatic successor to the diocesan bishop, had penned me a pastoral note, after my second rejection, similarly signed. It was a condolence note like you write when someone dies. But I had not yet died to the church. Arthur's was the only expression of empathy from on high, and I kept it—in Christ.

Dick and I hadn't planned our commandment breaking in the way you plan a vacation, figuring out the costs and making an itinerary. We'd fallen into what began as emergency love, love you don't decide on but you can't not follow, because the heart needs it so badly. Although now we were both divorced, clergy divorces were not considered an attractive alternative to anything. I'd already been bounced twice from the ordination process. This symphony date could risk a third strike against me.

At the symphony we settled into our seats and looked forward to hearing André Watt playing Tchaikovsky's First when Dick reacted to a sudden sharp pain in his left arm. "Hey let go of my arm," he hissed in my ear.

"Shhh. It's the bishop. Eleven o'clock northwest," I said tightening my grip.

"Let go," Dick said.

"Shhh. We should get out of here."

"But it's André Watt," Dick said.

I loosened my hold, feeling relieved—until Arthur Walmsley and his wife sat down in the row right behind us. The lights dimmed. My impulse was to run but the amazing Watt was programmed after the intermission. Then the opposite tactic arose in my mind.

"Dick, we should be mature. At intermission let's just greet the Walmsleys cordially as if we were, you know, normal."

"We are normal," Dick said. "So we'll stay in our seats."

"But I have to go."

"Hold it."

So we stayed in our seats. We sat straight, not daring to turn around or shift our butts. When the lights went on for the intermission, I felt as if they were spotlights on us. We looked straight ahead and didn't even whisper, except Dick murmured a couple of times, "André Watt."

The flying fingers of André Watt and the passion of Tchaikovsky swept us into wonder. When it was time to rise up with everyone else, clap, and cheer bravo, bravo, we jumped to our feet with the crowd. I sneaked a peak at Arthur, who was tapping his fingers lightly. On the way home Dick and I talked about André Watt, not Arthur Walmsley.

CHAPTER 9 Loving Alkies

"I need a job," I told my Crock-Pot, which I now envied for its utter insouciance. It was useless except to cook, so I called my faithful, ornery sister, Laurie, who had stood by me through all my trials.

"What about the Hartford Hospital chaplaincy?" she asked.

"The paid chaplaincy internship was only two years. It's over. Besides, I don't like the hospital setting for ministry—too touch and go," I said. "People get well and leave, or die and leave."

"It's a hospital," she said. "But didn't that pastoral counseling guy"— the interim supervisor in the hospital chaplaincy program—"offer you some counseling work? He must have thought you were good enough just by how you were with the patients and their families. Right?"

"Yes, but it's only part time. Not enough money," I said.

"Marry Dick. It works for love *and* money," she said.

"I'm not ready for marriage," I said.

"You think too much. So check the want ads."

"What church advertises in the want ads?" I said.

"Hey, you're calling yourself Lynnie Layperson now, so get off it and give up on the damn church," she said.

I pored over the C section of the want ads: cook, chef, computer, convenience store, clock repair*man*, carpenter —everything but cave*man*. I crumpled the paper and was about to toss it when my eye caught another C word: chaplain, part- to full-time position at BlueRidge, a newly opened alcohol and drug treatment center in Bloomfield, Connecticut. "Ordained" wasn't one of the qualifications. Against my sister's sound advice, I sat down to think.

Alcohol and drugs? Was drinking a sin? Whose drinking? This sin thing was complicated—not just one immoral act, or two or three, but a whole bag of down-deep tricks. How much of a sin was alcohol? Well, there was Uncle Jack, Dad's oldest brother, but he was an alcoholic. He went to Alcoholics Anonymous and always carried a huge thermos of coffee—a stand-in for the pocket flask he used to carry. He was tall with slumped shoulders, slick blue-black hair, a body like a vee, and a fun-house laugh. All the men in Dad's family drank a lot, but Jack, it was said, went "overboard" and *had* to join AA—a "punishment" Jack seemed to love. He talked about AA meetings and his meeting buddies with affection. Was Jack the only family alcoholic, or just the worst one? Damn, all of us could be Uncle Jacks. Was I, too? I made myself a cup of coffee, toasted Uncle Jack, and dialed the contact number in the ad.

The BlueRidge job was part time. It was a hospital but different. All the patients had the same diagnosis: addiction. They first underwent medical detoxification with the help of Valium. Then they stayed for four weeks. There was time to get to know people. Each patient had her or his individual counselor. Patients attended Alcoholics Anonymous meetings on site and other groups to educate them, medically, psychologically, and spiritually, about their disease—causes, treatment, relapse prevention, and maintaining sobriety one day at a time.

I got the BlueRidge job over other more qualified applicants for three reasons: I told the clinical director I didn't know much about alcoholism but I was a virgin, open to learning; when asked about my religious faith and compared to a nurse whom they'd just hired whose Christianity was studiously joyful, I said I thought my Jesus had more dirt under his fingernails than hers did; I lobbied against a proposed change of job title. They wanted to call me Pastoral Counselor, and I persuaded them to stick with what they'd advertised, Chaplain. Chaplain had a spiritual tone but trumpeted no religious particularity. My job responsibilities would be counseling individuals, running patient groups, especially on spirituality, and attending staff meetings and meetings with my own supervisor. I was to explain the spiritual components of addiction—basically explain God without mentioning God's name lest it offend or excite anger. I had big ideas, but first I had to steep myself in reading about addictions and the Twelve Steps of recovery, the third of which was an invitation to turn one's will and life over to the care of "God as we understood Him"—masculine gender a given, like in the church.

BlueRidge gave me a book called *Not God,* all about how bad "God" was for alkies. It was really about being sensitive to ways in which people with alcoholism had been shamed by self-righteous church/religion addicts who used the name of God for their own ends. Was God the problem or was it the church's patriarchal portrait of God? The Bible couldn't be blamed because it had every portrait you could think of in it—nothing you could nail down as absolute, which is precisely what makes the annoying book holy. AA's Bible, the Big Book, was filled with personal stories of hope and despair that I found moving—and familiar. I attended AA meetings and heard more grace-filled stories of second and third chances than I did in church. I noticed that meetings ended with the Lord's Prayer. AA called God Higher Power, so I did too.

Because of the nature of this job, alcohol-related memories occupied my mind. Why had I talked so much to God under the table about Dad's martini glass? Every man I'd ever loved—grandfather, father, uncles, husband, lovers, and sons—drank too much. But was this alcoholism? And what about the women? Dad's mother could kill you with a look and Aunt Sis made jokes about drunks, but neither drank. Mom, who had taken up wine after she turned forty, and I had enjoyed sitting together at the Sunday dinner table after my father and Bill left with their bottle to watch TV. We'd finish a bottle of wine, talk, and feel close in ways we didn't otherwise. I remembered hitting Bill with my leather boot, so hard he'd fallen back against the closet door. I was drunker than he was. Alcohol in my life had been a destroyer of relationships and a savior, a lubricant for intimacy and its murderer.

My first patient I'll call Noelle, although almost thirty years later I still remember her name. I went to see her in the detoxification unit and greeted her with a bright smile. She greeted me with a blast: "Get the fuck out of here, you fucking religious freak." Horrified, I obeyed. My staff community reminded me that she was feeling the tortures of alcohol's most brutal backlash: withdrawal.

"Dried out," Noelle was calmer. "It was that tiny cross around your neck. It looked huge to me," she said. "My mother used to throw God and church at me all day, then beat me up at night."

I took off my cross and gave it to her to inspect.

"Kinda pretty," she said. "Small too. But it's different. It has a hole in it. That's where the dead body's supposed to hang isn't it?"

"Yes, usually. What do you think?"

She fingered the cross and held it up.

"Want to try it on?"

"Nope. It's yours." She handed it back. "What does the body-shaped hole mean?"

"That God can take us off our crosses and help us heal."

"Just like that?"

"With your help. But you gotta follow God off the cross, which for you now is the pain of your alcoholism. Living without alcohol will feel like another cross for a while."

"I can't imagine life without alcohol to stop the pain," she said.

"You won't be alone. You'll have AA meetings, lots of buddies who know what it's all about, and listen to you forever, like the best family you can imagine."

My first patient—I'd worn a cross and used God's real name—and I'd survived. Maybe religion wasn't as much of a problem as I'd been told. I decided to keep wearing my cross, fucking religious freak or not.

For a disease alcoholism was strange. You didn't contract it via germs or viruses, and there was no cure for it, no medications except, well, love, support, and abstinence. It reminded me of the biblical stories of possession and exorcism. Jesus wasn't afraid of raving maniacs, but instead healed them of their diseases without judgment. Patients talked ceaselessly about failed efforts to control alcohol use. Failure and shame had taken over their souls and needed to be exorcised before they could imagine themselves lovable—by God or anyone. As I listened I felt my own shame, like a red-hot furnace on my face. Classical theological thought considered shame dangerous, a sure lead-in to sin. The downward spiral made sense to me, because how could you ever feel good about yourself, or know that God loved you, if you kept doing the same thing over and over and feeling worse and worse about yourself?

It was my job to help patients crawl out of the shame ditch, persuade them that Higher Power loved them, and that God's benevolent will was better for them than their own. I wondered if that idea couched healing in the language of willpower and thereby set up a power struggle with God. It sounded graceless.

Then I met Johnnie, a youth just twenty, with a long and successful drinking career.

"They said to see the chaplain," he said. "Make me believe in God."

I was supposed to be an expert, show him my stuff. I thought of feigning powerlessness to be in solidarity. But you *are* powerless, flashed through my mind.

"Do you want to believe in God?" I asked.

"Nope, but they say it's how I get well. I never heard of God before, to tell you the truth, chaplain," he said.

"You never heard of God?"

"Nope," he said.

Well, close my mouth. I'd never heard of anyone who'd *never* heard of God. Johnnie wasn't hostile, just blank. So I started to explain God, preached my fool head off, and felt empty. Never ever try to explain God, unless you want someone to come and surgically untie your foolish tongue. Johnnie and I sat silent for a while.

"Have you ever prayed?" I asked Johnnie.

"Nope. What's that?" he said.

I felt angry about this impasse, and it charged me up. "Okay," I said. "Listen. Have you ever felt all alone and scared and completely helpless, so desperate you called out—maybe out loud?"

"Yup. Lots."

"Well, who did you imagine you were calling?"

He sat up in his chair and leaned forward. "Is that God? Really?"

Good as any God I could think of. Johnnie's whole tragic tale spilled out. He used to go into the woods behind his house and scream his self-condemnations to the night. He talked and I listened. I had many visits with Johnnie. I don't know what became of him. He reminded me that there is no wrong—or right—way to pray. At that surprising moment I remembered the other shame lesson I'd learned from classical theology: shame, though dangerous when it takes hold, can also be a forerunner to a positive rearticulation of one's life. Mine or Johnnie's, I wondered?

"Wasn't he affable tonight?" my paternal grandmother once commented about a son-in-law in the sauce. Everyone sitting at the dining room table she presided over eagerly agreed. Stricken with my own soft spot for men who drank too much, I saw myself in a new light. From my father on, I'd tried to take care of these men, loving them to the point of losing myself. Shame about this failure told me that I needed a drink too. AA called this reasoning "stinkin' thinkin.'"

There was a program for the likes of me and my shame. At my first AlAnon and ACOA (Adult Children of Alcoholism) meeting, all I could think was *My mother would kill me if she knew I was here.* I learned you didn't have to drink to have alcoholism. Literature was flooding the market on a new "disease" called codependency. One hot-cake book was entitled *Women Who Love Too Much.* Of course a book about men would never get a title like that one, even if it addressed the same subject.

Setting aside my politics, I attended a workshop led by ACOA guru Janet Woititz. She tossed out symptom after symptom: reactivity (under or over), negativity, enabling, denial, lying, people-pleasing, overwork, secrecy, toxic shame, passive aggression, excited misery, and other addictions, including religiosity. The worst of the worst was called caretaking. I had them all. "It isn't even love you know, just sick codependency" she shouted at us. Who would dare ask a question? God, I'd rather be an alcoholic than a codependent.

"Write down a theme feeling, one you've felt on and off most of your life," Woititz instructed us. I wrote *inadequate* without a blink. When was a first time I'd felt it (at the cocktail hour when I was three) and more recently (at the Committee One interviews). I got the connection. Inadequacy and its solvent caretaking worked together to make addiction—dependence. Paradoxically, in the beginning alcohol (my father's) had led me to God, and moreover, alcohol led women into the prohibition movement (a failed attempt to control the uncontrollable), which empowered them to create the political suffragette movement. Were they trying to control their men or empower themselves? Was codependence a gender affliction or a gender gift, I wondered?

I didn't agree with Woititz about caretaking not being love. There was love in my motives, side by side with control. Motives are never singular. The thought of tough love, alone as a focus, chilled me. My efforts to love away addiction hadn't worked, and neither had Mom's. But we did truly love, and why should we be shamed for trying?

Debbie, a client at the pastoral counseling center job my Hartford Hospital supervisor had offered and I'd accepted, grew up with an alcoholic father. She had a habit of calling herself an "asshole codependent" because, as a child, she'd lost sleep and almost flunked out of school taking care of her father and her home. She'd force herself to stay awake until he came home drunk, cooked eggs, lit a cigarette or three, and passed out in a chair.

Then Debbie went to work tiptoeing around cleaning the kitchen, turning off the stove, and putting out the butts. Debbie's later alcoholism developed in part to quench the deep shame she felt over her caretaking behavior that had caused her to lose sleep. Her mother and sister slept through it. Debbie was the only one in her family who cared, for God's sake. Once sober, she'd sought counseling for her shame—not about her own drinking but about her "asshole" caretaking.

Tired of her "asshole" litany, tired of being understanding, I blurted, "You weren't an asshole, you were the savior!"

After a long pause Debbie broke into a gruff laugh. "An exhausting job, right?"

"But you did it for love, didn't you?"

"I guess I did," she said.

"So apply some of that love to yourself," I said. "You gotta look deeper than some label, deeper even than consequences if you want to be free. Look for the spiritual motivation. Yours was love."

Seeing clients and patients, many of them women, I developed some definitions of my own. What if behavior that looks sick and self-defeating is really an attempt at healing, soul-motivated by love? When people married more than one alcoholic seeking to right a wrong or heal a wound, psychology diagnosed their motivation "repetition compulsion," doing the same thing over and over, yet expecting different results. Insane, right? Yet I noticed that what some sane counselors called repetition compulsion in their clients, they called determination in themselves. Or what some counselors called resistance in a patient, they called good boundaries in themselves. Debbie's spiritual motivation had been sacrificial love. She'd complicated her own life to assure the safety of her family—and she was only a kid. I know there are unhealthy extremes to such heroics, and that caretaking should be balanced between self and other, but that doesn't mean the effort isn't rooted in love. This might have been risky thinking but it wasn't stinkin'. When I helped people see their deepest motivations I felt like a priest, consecrating the holy deep.

At BlueRidge I was becoming a good priest, ordained or not. This conviction, oddly, resulted in my thinking less not more about ordination. I began to make BlueRidge my parish, a community where I practiced a ministry of Word and Sacrament. I saw patients grab for "heaven" against "hellish" odds—and keep trying. Patients seemed to crave religion and its practices. Only once did a patient confront me with rage when I quoted from Proverbs, "The fear of God is the beginning of wisdom." Scared witless I stood up to him: "Fear means awe and reverence, God is Higher Power, and wisdom means you need to stay sober, Mister. So do I." He grinned. Patients flooded my office on Ash Wednesday to get their foreheads smeared with ashes in the sign of the cross and hear the familiar liturgical words, *Remember that you are dust and to dust you shall return.* I asked one man why he came." Oh, I dunno," he said. "Guess it keeps me humble. Silly, really."

I often retold the parable of the Prodigal Son who squandered his inheritance ("on alcohol" they all shouted, with guffaws and nodding grins), ended up eating with the swine, had a memory of family love, "came to himself," and returned to his father's home, where he was embraced. "This is what God is like," I'd say. "You can come home. The story doesn't say the son returned home sane and sober and all cleaned up, does it?"

"Shit no," one patient called out. "He was stinking of pig poop and he couldn't even eat pork!" All the patients roared.

Some might say I was playing church. But I wasn't a child. I was a hopeful, realistic woman. I wanted them to know the God I knew. I couldn't celebrate Eucharist with the patient community, but I was their "chaplain priest"—a little preaching, a few blessings, a dollop of sane theology, humor, prayers, even a weekly gathering I called The Community Spiritual Hour. I designated my office as the Meditation Room and set it up with a prayer rug, fake floral arrangements, and a comfortable chair. Nobody used it, but it was there, unlocked and waiting.

I knew this wasn't a parish church, just a darn good dress rehearsal. I felt fully alive.

CHAPTER 10 Three Strikes I'm Out?

Dick and I were in Boothbay Harbor, Maine, beguiled by the late summer beauty and the scent of pine, when our perpetual four-year-old fight erupted. Avoiding town for fear of seeing a bishop, we were walking in the woods. I kept my eyes peeled for scarlet shirts—the in-case-I-get-ordained symptom. We weren't married and my fear/faith quotient remained wobbly. The church wanted women with clerical collars to also have ringed fingers—to be married. I was afraid of marriage; more correctly, I did not trust myself to love enough. "Love and marriage / horse and carriage." The two go together, the song said. It wasn't even a hymn and I believed it. The pairing was almost biblical: God loved the people first and then made a covenant, a contract with expectations for both parties. It seemed simple.

There's no better place to fight than the woods in Maine. The high-rising evergreens provide a canopy that cools the heat of anger, permits no echo, and keeps the bright sun from bleaching the conflict; layers of pine needles slide and crackle underfoot, muffling sound like any good carpet.

"Why don't you want to get married?" Dick asked, once again.

"I do, or I might, I'm just not ready yet," I answered, once again.

"That's what you always say. When will you be ready, Lyn?"

"If I knew the answer to that I'd be ready, for God's sake."

Dick turned and walked off angry. I kept going, stopping after a while to listen for his footfall on the pine needles. Silence. I walked and walked, taking pleasure in crushing millions of needles and feeling furious at my own brain for failing to contrive a sound rationale for my hesitation. Marriage seemed like a trap, a forever trap—I would never risk another divorce. I balked at love: did I have it, could I do it, and what even was marital love anyway?

How can I not get married and still keep this man? What should I do, God? I yelled into the vast green silence.

By the time I returned to our cabin, it was darkening, the air cool. I opened the door and saw Dick reading on the bed. This infuriated me—he should have been pacing. True love would have paced. He looked up, cocked his head in the way he does when he wants to endear himself but doesn't know what to say.

"Will you?" I blurted.

"Marry me?" he said.

"No."

"What then?"

"Will you wait?"

I hadn't planned my bold query. It just popped out. I looked at Dick. He just sat there. Immediately visions of the vast marketplace of lonely single women tormented me—and Dick ready for marriage.

Finally he spoke. "Sure," he said, and stood to give me a hug.

"Sure? That's all?" I said. I can be so difficult.

"Lynnie, I love you. Sit down and listen for a change. After I walked back I settled down inside myself and decided to abandon my impulse, which was to issue some dramatic ultimatum like it's now or never, so . . ."

"You were thinking now or never?" I hadn't thought of that danger.

"I love you. I don't merely want to marry you." he said.

"Okay. Thanks. I love you too," I said, feeling relieved for my reprieve but still not sure what would set me free to marry—unless the truth I'd spoken actually would. "What shall we eat tonight?" I said, thinking how hunger so easily and often follows love. I felt a surge of joy at the thought that my three little words, *Will you wait?* ranked among the most faithful words I'd ever spoken. "It's light enough. Let's take a canoe ride to celebrate," I said.

"Celebrate what, my immaculate patience?" he said.

We pell-melled down to the small dock, hopped into a canoe, and paddled out. Neither of us knew anything about canoeing, but Dick said it was easy. We headed straight out, even picked up speed, when . . .

BRAAART.

I jumped. "There's an ocean liner right behind us," I yelled.

We were about to die before we had a chance at marriage.

"Paddle," Dick ordered from the rear.

I switched sides, sprinkling him, then dipped in and paddled mightily.

"No!" he screamed. "Not that way. We're spinning in a circle. Jesus Christ."

I couldn't help bursting into laughter. Then, with only Dick paddling, we moved ahead and escaped disaster. The cruise ship sounded a light tap on its monster horn and passed us by inches, or so it looked. The captain and crew members waved laughing their fool heads off. So we didn't save ourselves after all.

"We can't even paddle our own canoe. How the hell are we going to get married?" I spit these words out between fits of giggles.

"I'll do the paddling," Dick shot back.

"Hell you will. Let's go out for dinner," I said.

Within a short time we were engaged.

Laurie was a couple years into her second marriage. I thought, not without a dollop of older sister critique, that she'd rushed into it, and she thought I was a fool to wait. We wrangled over our differences but managed to stay sisters, so when I was thinking seriously of trying the ordination process, *again*, she bashed me *again*: "Shit, you're not. . . . You are such an asshole. Oh my God, Lynnie." Laurie was nothing if not blunt, so I could trust her never to waffle.

"I know I've done everything you did, only three years later. But I'm telling you, this is one damn idiotic thing I'm never doing!" she said.

"Well, you got remarried three years *before* me," I said.

"Yes, but I wasn't marrying the rector, and thinking I'd get ordained," she said.

"But this is a new bishop. The church is all politics, you know. Hey, have you seen the movie *Flashdance*? It's my favorite flick of all time. I've seen it twice. It's—"

"Please don't tell me it's about a priest or some Salomé of religion."

"No, its about a woman welder whose also a wannabe dancer. She puts on hot rock music and writhes around, performing for her grunty boxer dog. She's dying to study at the elite Pittsburgh ballet school . . ."

"Yeah, like the church," Laurie said.

"Shut up. The girl gets an audition. She wows the ballet committee with her wild dancing. They tap their old fogey feet and fingers in spite of themselves. She gets in."

"So you're going to dance for another church committee? They won't tap their feet, I promise you," Laurie said.

Only Dick thought this third try was a good idea. I prayed and got sick of squint-work discernment. God was silent. I wondered, would Arthur of the symphony even see me? I cast myself as victim, fool, or bad girl, until I remembered my dream image in which I was cast as the biblical king David, an unlikely candidate for divine favor—adulterer, murderer, failed parent, a mess. But David was Jesus' ancestor and so vulnerable with shame and sorrow it could break even the hardest heart. I wrote one clear-hearted prayer: Soften this new bishop's heart toward me. Over and over I wrote the same until one day God's familiar bemused voice within interrupted: *Lyn, I don't care if you're ordained.*

I dialed the number of the bishop's office, and got an appointment with Bishop Walmsley. His office was welcoming. We sat in chairs living room style—no great massive desk between us.

"So what brings you here?"

Didn't he know? Arthur looks a lot like the ninety-eighth Archbishop of Canterbury, William Temple. I'd taken a course on Temple's *Nature, Man and God,* published in 1935. I'd read it all, understood half, and thought the teacher was boring. But Temple had fire in the belly. He would've known why I was here. Still, I had to say it myself—possibly what Arthur wanted.

"Well, I still feel strongly called, by God of course, to be a priest. As you know, I was turned down for postulancy, but I thought there might be a chance to try again." Then I exhaled.

Arthur leaned so far back in his swivel chair, I worried he'd tip over. The body language suggested he might like to flee the scene. He adjusted his perfectly round-framed pre-Harry Potter glasses and cleared his throat.

I raced on. "I never got a chance to thank you for the kind note you sent after I was turned down. It was so . . ."

"Yes, you're welcome. Such things are painful, but I thought we might talk a bit about the symphony concert where I saw you and Dick Simeone."

Arthur Walmsley remembered André Watt.

"Yes, André Watt. Wasn't it wonderful?" I said.

"When I saw you two there, I was furious."

Oh God, what do I say? If only Dick, Mr. Cool-in-a-Collar, was here. Arthur, the bishop who disliked *ad hominem* rhetoric could himself have *ad hominem* reactions.

"Yes, we love the symphony," I said. (It's not always true what the Bible says about the Holy Spirit sending you the right words.)

After a pause, Arthur continued. "What do your colleagues say about you two? Aren't they angry?"

"I don't think so. Dick and I are both divorced now."

"Yes, I find it distressing. All this divorce. Clergy."

Was he telling me he had no idea what to make of divorce? If I thought about it, I wouldn't either.

"I just don't like messes." Arthur's frank disclosure endeared him to me. I was presenting him with a mess, yet he didn't make me feel messy.

"Change is hard, and the whole women's ordination issue is still so new. It must be hard to adapt." A subtle change of subject—the Holy Spirit came through this time, made me a good little pastor.

Another adjustment of the glasses. "Well, perhaps we should talk about why you feel called to the ordained ministry, Lyn."

It was time for my elevator speech: "A former rector encouraged me, and a seminary professor told me I had a solidly traditional vocation. (I didn't tell him the professor was Roman Catholic.) I am drawn to priesthood to celebrate the Eucharist. I know there are other things that go into it, but that is what always emerges most strongly for me."

"Yes, that's pretty minimalist. I'd like to hear more of your story, though. Why don't we schedule some meetings to talk. Ruth takes care of my calendar, so she'll schedule you in." He got up and extended his hand. Our meeting was over.

Ding?

My meetings with Arthur Walmsley over the course of a year were among the best gifts I received from the church and religion. I told him about my spirituality and early sense of call under the dining room table, about my first marriage and the role of alcohol in my life, and about seminary and my learnings (omitting the sexual ones). I did most of the talking in response to his questions. It was hard to tell exactly what Arthur thought, but I guessed he found me credible. Most importantly he listened and when Dick and I went together to tell him we were to be married he was delighted. Well, of course—me legitimized.

We chose November 23, 1986, by the liturgical calendar. Christ the King Sunday is the last before the beginning of a new liturgical year in Advent. (To those like me who bristle at male monarchy as metaphor for

God, I'd say that if Christ is king, at least no one else can be, and that Christ, like God, is not a boy's name.)

"Okay, king Christ, but no *Diademata*," I said. ("Crown Him with Many Crowns" is the traditional hymn for that Sunday.) "One crown is enough."

We had picked the date for its message: God can make happy endings out of the worst human messes and wrest life out of any kind of death, including divorce. The parish church would be dressed up for hope in the God of reversals and second chances. What about third chances? I'd need a third to get ordained. I didn't know if we could do marriage well, but I knew Dick.

Our wedding was a clergyperson's dream—no white billowing gown with a train to get twisted, no giddy young bridesmaids teetering down the aisle in stiletto heels, no ogling groomsmen with beer breath, no aggressive wedding planner trying to position the priest, no need to persuade doting daddies that fathers do not "give" their daughters away, and no need to explain why Wagner's Wedding March from *Lohengrin* to announce the bride's grand entrance would not be played—it's not sacred music, and few people of boomer generation hear it without thinking "Here comes the bride, fair, fat and wide."

We walked together down the aisle and married according to the Episcopal prayer book's sacramental rite, The Celebration and Blessing of a Marriage. He, the Rev. Richard John Simeone, called Dick, and I, the not-yet-Rev. Lynda Hall Gillespie Brakeman, called Lyn, said our vows at a parish Eucharist. Trinity's Priest Associate officiated. Our guests, besides family and a few friends, were parishioners. Dick had been Trinity's rector for eight years and I, despite my checkered career, still hoped Trinity loved me.

When I said my marriage vows the first time, I was twenty-three and paralyzed by performance anxiety. I'd ridden up the aisle on the crest of my mother's ecstasy; I didn't yet have my own travel feet. I clung to my father's arm, grateful for its steady bend. Bill and I must have looked like plastic bride and groom statuettes secured on a wedding cake of dreams by the sticky sweet icing, not a terribly accurate depiction of marriage. I've often wondered if Bill felt as frightened and unprepared as I did.

When I said the marriage vows a second time, I was forty-eight and, despite some normal-for-me fear, actually knew what I was doing. Dick and I looked at each other. I faltered in tears. Public vows are so . . . public. Dick's mustache quivered slightly. I knew my tears looked awful.

I wondered if they had something to do, once again, with my mother. Dick doesn't look at all like Bill or Dad, Mom's prizes. When I'd told her Dick and I had decided to marry, she shrugged, took a bite of her salad, smiled sourly, and said, "I want you to be happy." It sounded like scant approval, so I pushed for more. "Oh, I like him all right" was all she gave. I'll never know what she really thought, but I did know I had finally made a life decision not under the influence—of alcohol or mother.

I married Dick for lots of reasons—good lovemaking, good fights, good humor, good cooking, good conversation, and good church. How many husbands would debate theology over the breakfast table? And Dick's laugh is like a sunburst—a laugh of abandon, almost as if his life depended on it. These for me were the things of love. Also, he had a Crock-Pot twice the size of mine.

The church's prayer for new couples says it all: "Make their love together a sign of Christ's love to this sinful and broken world, that unity may overcome estrangement, forgiveness heal guilt, and joy conquer despair." Pretty idealistic vision, but it reflected what the bishop who'd interrogated us after we got caught had said. "If your love is in Christ it will prevail."

Arthur and I had one more meeting scheduled. His biggest concerns were "my history"—having been turned down twice by his predecessor—and his distaste for "messes." We both knew what mess we were circling.

What you yourself don't put on the table of truth, someone else usually will. The former rector of my fieldwork parish had an extramarital affair with a female parishioner in his new parish in another diocese. It had nothing to do with me, but it pushed Arthur's fear/wrath/mess buttons, mostly because the errant couple fled and landed back in Connecticut on Arthur's Episcopal lap. This development brought our conversations to a halt. Arthur said he appreciated my candor and would send me a letter soon. I worried, no, panicked. The impact and timing of these twin disturbances could exceed the limits of this bishop's human goodness and pastoral office. I almost felt sorry that the church received so many assaults on its moral stances in such a short time.

In two weeks Arthur's letter arrived. I put it on the kitchen counter, where it sat for several minutes. I held it up to the light, weighed it in my hands. Rejection letters are short and heftless. Vowing bravery, I opened it.

The letter was one whole page, single-spaced. Arthur had decided that because of my "history" and the current clergy divorce issue, he could not admit me to the ordination process. Bravery vanished. Something detonated inside me. Strike three. I was out. No third chance.

I called Laurie who came racing to the rescue. She held onto me and didn't say "I told you so." Everyone but Dick declared it a lost cause.

"Let me read that letter," he said.

"I've read it over and over," I moaned.

"No, you have not. Listen to the closing sentence. 'If you have questions and want to discuss this matter further, please call Ruth to make an appointment to see me.' There's a loophole. Call Ruth."

"Again?"

"Why not?" Dick said. "He didn't say 'Stay outta my life, Lyn.' He didn't say you didn't have a call to priesthood. He said call Ruth."

"*If* I had questions and wanted to discuss. What's to discuss? More wannabe priest-chick?" I said.

Dick just looked at me as if to say, *well?* But a fourth storming of the diocesan Bastille?

I needed a priest. I'd never experienced the sacrament of Reconciliation of a Penitent—confession. My Protestant-trained mind had associated this rite exclusively with stories of Catholic kids making up sins every week to satisfy Father, who doled out absolutions and penances by the dozens, then wearily waited until next week to hear Suzie Q again confess that she'd fought with the same sister from the week before. Episcopalians say a general confession every Sunday and receive collective absolution. Too generic. I needed big guns. There was something compelling about the structure of formal liturgical language and the touch of hands to confer the grace— God's, not ours—of forgiveness. It cut into sin's possessive power.

"Bless me for I have sinned," the penitent begins. I began.

"I confess to Almighty God, to his Church, and to you, that I have sinned by my own fault in thought, word and deed, in things done and left undone; especially . . ."

I had a whole list, but after "especially" said "I committed adultery." This seemed to sum it up.

My confessor, an Episcopal priest, was a very tall, serious man who listened, asked no questions, and gave no advice as I filled in details, clumsily. I knew his long arms would reach as I knelt before him and bent my one small head. "Our Lord Jesus Christ, who offered himself to be sacrificed for us to the Father, and who conferred power on his Church to forgive sins, absolve you through my ministry by the grace of the Holy Spirit, and restore you in the perfect peace of the Church. Amen. The Lord has put away all your sins." The priest concluded, as it is written, with a most graceful sentence. "Go in peace, and pray for me, a sinner."

I called Ruth and got an appointment later than sooner.

When I again sat waiting for Ruth to summon me forth, I asked and answered myself: *Why do you want to stay in this storm-tossed relationship with the church?* Where else can I go to soak in Mystery? The church is the guardian of God-stuff.

"The bishop will see you now, Lyn."

Our conversation was stilted. Arthur delivered his own elevator speech. "So, Lyn, the fact is that I just can't admit you to the ordination process in Connecticut. You have many gifts and are honest and feel called by God, but I am responsible for the church's call and . . ."

I felt like a dog about to whimper after making a mess on the rose-beige carpet.

"Bishop Walmsley," I began, "I think you should reconsider. I'm ready to take authority as a priest in the church of God."

My voice was clear, noncombative, not *ad hominem*-ish. I don't remember my exact words—just the case I made. What about the gospel of forgiveness? I've made a million bad moves and I'm sorry. I've made my confession and received sacramental absolution. My seminary record is excellent. I've been found fit in all the required categories and have met the standard of learning. I've been wounded enough psychologically and pastorally by the church's fearful attitudes about women, yet I've never denied my vocation. I will be a good priest. I want to take the church's word and sacraments to the people who feel lost and outcast, like the patients at BlueRidge.

Arthur listened.

I went on. "And what about my home parish, the people of Trinity and my family too, who now think the church is not only wrong but power hungry? They put me forward and their judgments have been discounted."

"You are the chief pastor. So Bishop, will you ordain me a priest?"

Arthur sat back, tilting and swiveling. I waited.

"Okay," he said. "I will bring your situation up to the Commission on Ministry. If they agree, we'll proceed to postulancy. Then you can take the canonical examinations, and if Committee Two passes you, I will ordain you deacon, then priest, since that is obviously your chosen vocation."

We shook on it. Thank you anointing woman—God and Jesus too.

On the way home I stopped at a phone booth to call Dick. "Hey. You won't believe this. I had a spiritual power surge, and Arthur said he'd ordain me. Seriously, he said he'd bring it up to the Commission on Ministry. He was about to turn me down again, but I busted out, felt like the anointing woman without nard or rage. Suddenly I had the skills of an attorney. Who do we know on that commission?"

"So he said he'd ordain you?"

"So yes. You doubt? Who's on the Commission?"

"Damn! Good girl. It's not over yet. I love you."

"Me too, I mean you. All politics, well, politics and prayer. Slap words like 'holy' or a 'sacred' onto it, fine, but politics is still politics. It motorizes everything," I said.

Although the heart of Dick's priesthood thrived on the drama of excellent liturgy and cannon-fodder justice preaching, he adored politics. He'd majored in political science at Brown and loved intrigue, behind-the-scenes massaging of attitudes, pastoral hobnobbing, and the excitement when an action that looked somewhat like the kingdom of God took hold.

"I'm calling Ann Coburn," I told him. "I think she's on the Commission. I need a woman."

"You don't think a man would be more effective? I mean, carry more weight?"

"Dick! Nope. A woman. Ann's the daughter-in-law of a bishop, and she's a priest, but not one Arthur had to decide on. She has clout and knows how the system works. I like her. Do you think it was the Holy Spirit roaring up inside me?"

"Nah. It was you, babe. Take the credit."

"You're too empirical. Okay, let's say we did it together."

"Who?"

"Dick! Me and the Holy Spirit. "

I called Ann the next day. She agreed to make sure Arthur brought up my name. I suddenly tasted the delicious flavor of solidarity and teamwork, the kind the "illegally" ordained women had enjoyed. Adversity is a petri dish for courage.

I had another shot at postulancy. I was nearing the end of a long journey. All I had to do was start at the beginning again: Committee One (different people this time), psychiatrist (different one), canonical exams, written and oral (taken five years after I'd graduated from seminary), Committee Two, which read and oversaw the examinations, diaconate ordination, and then finally, finally I would be ordained priest in the church of God.

CHAPTER 11 Flying Up

In an hour I'd have the "brass ring" I'd always wanted and been afraid to grab for as I'd spun round the church's mazes. My ring wouldn't be brass or gold but it would be round—a clerical collar and the sacramental authority of the office of priest it symbolized. The official religious ordination meant gender justice and public power and authority bestowed on a woman in the patriarchal church of my choice. God had listened to me as a kid, and all along—not to do my bidding but to shape my soul, so that, gradually, I recognized a vocation and the gift that, to me, made it unique. One of the acts a priest does is to consecrate, to make sacred, to signal the presence of divine grace buried in the ordinary. To consecrate with integrity, I think, you first have to ken the holy, have faith in the grace of it, then call it forth and share it round. That's what I did with the Ritz crackers under the table forty-seven years ago.

The church would declare itself aloud today. Today it was all here—every hope, every beauty, every wish and prayer, all the things that had captivated my imagination since childhood.

Breathless with excited anxiety I stood in the narthex of Trinity church and inhaled the aroma of dozens of roses, red, pink, yellow, and white, coming from the sanctuary—scents of a woman. I looked down at my feet. They got me here. Would they propel me forward?

A quick inventory reassured me that Bishop Walmsley was present. I shot him a glance, but he wasn't looking my way. He was absorbed in retrieving a handkerchief from a pocket under his layers of sacred vestments, just in time to catch a loud sneeze. Arthur had a serious, nose-dripping cold—but he was here and ready. Without him to represent the authority of the whole church, the sacramental action and august pronouncement that would make me a priest wouldn't happen.

I took my position in line just ahead of the bishop who ditched his handkerchief, donned his mitre, and thumped his crozier thrice on the floor. The narthex was carpeted but you'd think it was an empty echoing hall with a bare stone floor the way my innards jumped. What if his crook circled my neck and held me back? The procession—long, stately, near-balletic—rivaled the academy for elegance. The crucifer led in. She was the young daughter of a friend. I watched as she carefully gripped the high, gleaming, gold processional cross, stacking her fists, heading in opposing directions for form and balance, one on top of the other. The choir in blue robes with white collars, two by two like ark passengers, walked next. Then came acolytes, the sister of the crucifer and her twin sisters, one my goddaughter, in red robes with white cottas. They were followed by their mother, the litanist with the luscious voice, and behind her, my presenters, Laurie and the priest at the parish where I'd served as a deacon, and then vested clergy (friends, supporters, witnesses, and relieved soul mates). Dick—preacher, emcee, parish rector, husband of ordinand—walked alone. So did the ordinand (me in my new white alb). Bringing up the rear strode the bishop, all in white, crozier in hand. We were truly a magnificent bunch. Dick turned to blow me an air kiss.

While we waited for our cue music, the opening hymn, I thought about pronouns to keep my nerves at bay. How astonishingly simple it had been to implement the historic vote that moved women from pew to altar and pulpit. They just had to italicize the men, so that *she* could be substituted for *he;* where *he* was. Of course it was clear whose pronoun was subsumed under whose. Yet here I was, the fullness of *she* within *he,* in 1988 about to walk with steady steps—proudly humble—up a straight aisle, ready for the right pronouns to make this rite right.

Swells of the grand Haydn hymn "The Spacious Firmament" crescendoed. As good as André Watt, I thought. I chose this creation hymn because it reminded me that male/female equity was ordained by divine design. The procession snaked slowly forward. The sanctuary was dressed up in Easter white. Inside I felt winged.

I looked down at my feet again, small, beautiful. Walk, I said; they walked—slowly one after the other.

The congregation was full of smiling faces, happy for me and happy they no longer had to ride the ordination merry-go-round with me. My mother sat in the front row, "bride's side." I could barely see her. She was small, swallowed by her fur jacket, seventy-six and bent with osteoporosis.

But she was smiling her pride-and-joy smile. I imagined she missed Dad, dead for just five years now. He'd be here if he could. I wondered if Mom thought of Jeanie, her absence leaving another hole in the fabric of the day.

My four children and Dick's three sat up front. They ranged in age from fifteen to twenty-five. I winked at them. Some grinned, some shes wept, and some hes looked straitjacket uncomfortable. Bored by the pageantry, they still were here, all of them, I imagined, filled with varying degrees of pride, love, and unresolved post-divorce resentments. They were here for me and for Dick. This time our four teenage sons couldn't sneak out as they had at the cathedral when I was ordained deacon in 1987. Today they were trapped loyalists—and well beloved for it.

Laurie stood before the bishop with other presenters and attested to my fitness. We'd rehearsed her lines. Laurie knew plenty of "impediments" in this candidate. But she did her part. I chose Laurie not out of sisterly duty but out of respect for her and for all we had been through together and would continue to go through. The church, according to her, was overly devoted to "vows, robes, and collars—not at the heart of anything concerning God, who calls everyone to serve." My path seemed to her like a "damn fool idea," as our dad would say. (Laurie talked like him and I had it down pretty well, too.) She ranted, and raved, and pretended to puke about the "screwed up" church "full of jackasses," then showed up and said exactly what she was supposed to, according to the rite. You do such things for intimate enemies you love.

Today was Mary's day, Feast of the Annunciation, March 25, and we would hear again the familiar Gospel story in Luke. I'd first become attached to Mary in a Roman Catholic church and on the streets in Spain. She was a statue and bad art but a woman up front in hearts as well as sanctuaries. As the biblical story goes, Mary, engaged but not wed, was visited by a large male angel named Gabriel who got her to agree to have sex—with the Spirit of God no less—and get pregnant. "Don't you need a man for that?" she asked—exactly what people said when women wanted to be priests. Mary got a trust me-like answer. Her story felt so familiar—breaking norms of church and society, hoping God, with the help of her womb and in my case a lot of sweat equity, would pull a reversal of norms. Fortunately, I didn't have to get pregnant for it.

In Dick's sermon he spoke about Mary and about priesthood, but directly to me. His homily, emotion in words, shot right into me. He stood before me, placed his trust in me, and made love to me right there in front of hundreds. A friend later said that she could see sparks between us, and Laurie said it was the only time she'd seen him "speechless." She told me that when he said "my sister" to me, she could see joy in our faces. "It was very moving and transparent, his caring for you and a joy on your face I couldn't remember seeing before," she told me. "I knew it was where you needed to be, no matter what I thought." To me, the moment felt as if Dick and I ascended together in a bubble yet stood solidly earthed. It was our love, our shared vocation, and something more.

The sermon moment was fleeting but its echoes carried me through the rest of the service and my vows. Vowing is hard. Solemn vowing was worse. I vowed to listen to my bishop, believe the Scriptures contained everything necessary to salvation, have an outstanding lifestyle, care for people without condition, pray, be a faithful minister of Word and Sacrament. This vowed life could be harder than marriage, and God might be impossible to divorce.

The ordaining moment was the climax of this rite. I called it the hands-on moment and thought it would make me real. What would it be like? People had told me something big would happen, but they never told me exactly what. The ordaining moment is physical. Bodies press against bodies. Bodies of clergy would surround me, overshadow me like a hood, and a dozen or more hands fall on my one small brown head. It was, I felt sure, the embodied way to say: *We all are here. We all are with you. Our heavy hands weigh in with warmth, encouragement, collegiality, love, and support.* These hands would be energetic vehicles of God's grace today as I became one of them. A more powerful swearing in I couldn't imagine.

It was time. I moved to stand in front of the bishop's lofty chair.

Dear God, help me get a little distance from this firestorm of vulnerability I'm in.

The clergy gathered round. I knelt in front of the bishop, a giant. I felt the body heat closing in, sensed the hands before they landed. I felt short, small, sinking and shrinking. I could hardly breathe. I couldn't see anything but the red carpet and the scene from Jesus' life that the altar guild women had labored to needlepoint onto my kneeler. I bowed my head and waited.

The bishop placed his hands on my head first, others followed, and the bishop intoned:

"Therefore Father, through Jesus Christ your Son, give your Holy Spirit to Lyn, fill her with grace and power, and make her a priest in your church." (No italics!)

The hands, almost as one, lifted.

My inner silence was absolute, complete. I felt my body gathered in and up. Thomas Merton, the twentieth-century monk and poet, might call this *le point vierge*, the virgin point, a point of nothingness and pure truth. I *did* feel nothing and everything at once. I thought it must be the way being conceived would feel, if we could feel it. Rather than the usual idea of God's spirit being planted in human flesh I had a sense of being planted inside God.

It was time to come to God's dining room table for Holy Eucharist. Eating is what people do at any occasion of love, solemn or joyous or both. They eat to show they're still alive and well and they still have each other. Many Christians do it every Sunday to re-member divine love. Proof of life. Sign of the Holy. We banquet.

As a newly ordained *she*-priest, my only liturgical role was to invite people to exchange a sign of Christ's peace (hugs all round) and say the final blessing. "The blessing of God Almighty, Father, Son, and Holy Spirit, be with you always."

I had quibbles with this language and image (too many *hes* in one holy triangle)—but not today.

秂

Two photos stood out when, months later, I pasted a colorful parade of images into the biggest scrapbook they had at the local discount store.

One pictured me on tiptoes, hugging Arthur at my diaconal ordination. He had listened to me when others of the hierarchy, which in the Episcopal Church isn't very high, had not. My midlife growth spurt alarmed him. It had alarmed me too, but at the time it didn't seem to be any more containable than God in a whirlwind. Despite the church's sexism and despite my own mid-life moral morass, I had become a priest. Institutions and individuals can mess up, be afraid, yet keep trying, even as they sin wildly. The photo exemplified this.

The other photo was snapped at the hands-on moment. According to the rules of this rite, only an Episcopal bishop and Episcopal priests are authorized to lay hands upon an ordinand's head when the sentence of ordination is pronounced and places the new priest into the historical succession of church leaders—a long line. But someone broke the rules. My supervisor at the pastoral counseling center, a United Church of Christ minister dressed in black academic gown with red velvet stripes on its sleeves, had wedged himself into the circle of Episcopal clerics robed in white albs and stoles. His outstretched hand was placed squarely and visibly on top of my head, "defiling" the "perfect" picture. Whether an act of defiance on his part or an act of caring solidarity, I didn't know; nor did I know who caught this hilarious moment. The photo prophesied what the future church might be, and poked fun at Episcopal hierarchical pretensions.

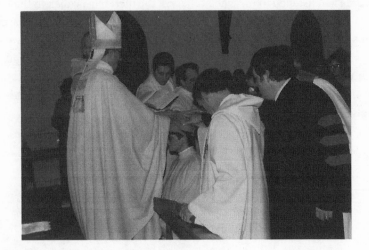

Lastly, I placed on the first scrapbook page my ordination bulletin, its cover calligraphed for the occasion by a monk of the Order of the Holy Cross, in blue on cream with words I'd chosen, words of Irenaeus, Bishop of Lyons in 178 CE. Irenaeus was responsible for locking Christian orthodoxy into patriarchal theology and the implacably male omnipotence of the Creator God, yet, ironically, he was also the one who risked his life defending Christian incarnational theology and wrote words that freed me to be a woman in Christ.

The glory of God is the human person fully alive.

On the day of my ordination I was a woman fully alive.

CHAPTER 12 Parochial Tryouts

The Sunday after I was ordained I would celebrate my first mass as a priest at Calvary Episcopal in Suffield where I'd served as a deacon for nine months. I dress-rehearsed at Trinity, with Dick as my priest-school teacher—my stance, the tilt of my head as I looked at the service book, the exact elevation of my arms, the projection of my voice, even my priestly garb, as I said the words of consecration over the invisible bread and wine.

"This is the moment when Jesus jumps into the bread," Dick said. "Don't muff it."

"And if I do, where will Jesus go? Into the wild blue yonder? I wish I were doing my first Eucharist here."

"Just think of me at your side," Dick said.

"No. I'll put you in a pew where I can see your grinning face. If you were beside me you'd be snatching things up and taking charge," I said.

"I would not! Well, only if I saw you about to make a mistake."

"Donatist," I said. (Donatism is an early church heresy, basically idolatrous perfectionism about the church and its liturgies.)

Our irreverent humor helped me to take my nervousness less seriously. It also helped me to say, out loud, the words I would say alone as a priest, elegant words so familiar I thought I should know them by heart, but didn't. As I recited them, my confidence rose—until I got to this line: "He stretched out his arms upon the cross, and offered himself, in obedience to your will, a perfect sacrifice for the whole world." I faltered. I'd heard it a million times. We'd parsed it in seminary and argued its merits and demerits, read the history and many erudite intellectual interpretations of this doctrine called atonement. For centuries it had been the church's way of understanding Jesus' death. It just didn't sound like God to me, to demand a price for love, but it was oh so traditional and ingrained in our

Christian brains, and I'd have to say it out loud. Thank God I'd be reading, not reciting. Memorization would have put these words into my heart—too close for my spiritual comfort.

"Keep going," Dick yelled from the back pew. "Your voice dipped."

"Do I have to believe everything I say up here?"

"Of course not. Welcome to the priesthood. Say it all again," he said.

"The revised prayer book should have softened this. It's unfair to God," I called back to him, then said the whole thing over twice more without hesitation. I was ready.

On Sunday morning I draped my stole over both shoulders. I squared my shoulders, enjoying the shoulder symmetry of a priest's stole. (The deacon's stole draped over one shoulder and across the front to fasten at my right hip.) Then I donned a voluminous chasuble over the whole outfit. It was made for me by a friend out of fabric covered with golden sheafs of wheat and lined in white; heavy, but it made me feel held—a very good thing indeed as it turned out. I was ready.

After the readings and the exchange of the peace, the rector welcomed the newly ordained priest. The applause died down, after which he made an announcement of his own: he would be having serious lung surgery, after which he would take a long sabbatical leave to recuperate. "Lyn will be in charge while I'm gone." People gasped. So did I. Two impulses twisted my gut: flattery at his trust of me and fury that he had not told me of this plan before this public minute. This was not the first time this man had done such a thing, but there was not time to indulge feelings. I had to step up to the plate, or the altar, and celebrate the Eucharist as smoothly as if I'd done it all my life—which in a way I had. I thought of Dick and the child under the table, and every gesture and all the words were pitch perfect.

"Did you know he was going to do this?" a woman with pure white hair, dressed in a stylish navy blue suit and print blouse, its collar peeping above the buttoned-to-the-top jacket, asked me in a gentle tone at the coffee hour. She did not wait for my answer but patted my arm.

God, I loved this woman, and God, I didn't know how to do this, but this was parish ministry and I felt I had to do it right. The bishop had said I must get a parish placement in addition to my jobs at BlueRidge and the pastoral counseling center. I'd vowed obedience to the bishop so here was my first obedience trial. I wondered whether I'd been part of this rector's sabbatical plan all along. Of course he couldn't have known he'd get cancer. Of course not.

"Remember how the rector introduced me to Calvary when I started there as a deacon? How he introduced this new deacon and the people didn't know I was coming?" I asked Dick when I got home.

"Yeah, but you'd felt so proud of that deacon's stole. You said it was just the opposite diagonal of Miss America's sash. Smashing, you said, and you were. So what happened today?"

"Right. Well, he did it again. He's leaving right away on sabbatical, plus lung cancer surgery, and guess who is in charge?" I said.

"You?" Dick started to laugh and stopped as he saw I was crying.

"I'm so angry," I stammered. "He never told me, and how can you get angry at a guy that might be dying?" I pushed Dick's hug aside. "Don't feel sorry for me. I can do it. This morning was amazing. I'm a priest now, and about to be almost a rector by default. The people will help me. I'll be smashing."

"Atta girl," he said.

"Preaching every week, by the way, scares me to death. I'll be part time of course but Sunday is more than part time all by itself. And me with three jobs miles apart. Also, I'm already afraid of Pete."

"Slow down. Who's Pete?'

"A man in the parish who hates women priests."

"You're focused on the biggest negative force in the parish. Look at the ones who smile and nod at you."

"Can't."

"Why?"

"Don't know. Pete's easier."

"You mean Pete's an old habit. Relax. I love you," he said, his love covering a multitude of sins—mine.

Pete, adamant and vocal about his opposition to women priests, was stuck with me if he wanted his Jesus food. Still, I worried about the daunting geographic distance and schedule: BlueRidge on Monday, Wednesday, and half of Thursday in Bloomfield, pastoral counseling on Tuesday and Thursday evenings in Glastonbury, and parish priest Monday evenings, Tuesdays, and Sundays in Suffield. I lived in Collinsville. Check your maps. It was the Bermuda triangle of lost clergy.

Anxiously eager and determined—and in for an unprecedented pastoral growth spurt—I leapt into parish ministry. I made pastoral calls, potentially awkward for an introvert who doesn't do small talk well. I learned I could be with people over tea and cookies, listen to them without, in most cases, having to counsel them—chat. Office hours were fun because I had my own very large desk. I was really the only staff. The music director came in to practice and filled the small church with hummable hymns—background music that soothed.

Monthly vestry meetings were all business—endless discussions about whether to spend $100 on a new lock for a door we never used, or so it seemed to me. I let the treasurer take the lead, which he loved to do anyway. Something, I'd noticed (even as a layperson in a small parish), can happen when corporate types get elected to run parish business; they lose their heads, let trivia become gospel. Do they think God might be watching? I tried to set a loving-God tone by insisting that we have silence and a brief meditation to begin each meeting. People were politely tolerant, but I could tell by the sighs and shuffling of papers during the silence that they preferred the usual token prayer from the prayer book, asking God for guidance so we could get on with it and do what we wanted.

The altar guild ladies were my biggest fans. They relished showing me the "correct" way to set the table, and, best of all, cleaned up and washed and ironed all the linens. They were the "wife" I didn't want to be. Preaching remained stressful. I would begin to prepare for next Sunday immediately on Monday morning. I sat at my desk at BlueRidge, skimmed the lectionary lessons, and jotted down some ideas so I knew I'd have something to say. I called this practice panicky *pre*crastination, doing today what really could have waited till at least tomorrow. Most clergy say they "pray" with the reading to prepare, but I wondered because so many left sermon prep to Saturday evening. In my sermons I never called God *He*. Some women loved my humor and my delicately nuanced feminist slants. Once I overheard Pete say, "She has a few good sermon points." I puffed up as if the Archbishop of Canterbury had paid me a compliment. I loved being a priest of the Eucharist, especially at the informal weekday Eucharist when we could have a conversation about the readings. The half dozen women who attended grew to expect the question I posed after the Gospel reading: "So what do you think?" They were all closet theologians—and good ones.

When the rector returned from his sabbatical in good remission I was startled by my instant relief. I'd loved the people and my newfound authority as a priest. I also knew I couldn't stay on. Besides the travel fatigue I harbored nagging doubts about whether I was really suited to be a parish priest full time. Was I a rector?

I left Calvary after two and a half years. They gave me a festive coffee hour, a kudos, and a wide white stole handmade by the same women who'd held me up and who have held up the church for centuries. Pete approached me and stood sideways in front of me. He cleared his throat, looked down at the floor, and said, "Well, you've converted me." I held out my hand for a manly handshake.

𝍐

In 1989 a heartening and astounding upset happened in the Episcopal Church. The diocese of Massachusetts elected the Rev. Barbara C. Harris to serve as suffragan bishop. Harris is an African American woman, diminutive in stature, expansive in spirit. This was gospel politics at its best. It was a profound offense to some and a great joy to others. I was in the great joy camp. The news sent me flying. I called Laurie.

"Hey, guess what Massachusetts just did? Practically lifted the old staid institutional church off its arse and threw it into a tailspin."

"What the hell are you talking about?" Laurie said, thinking me nuts as usual.

"They elected a woman bishop, black no less. A WOMAN! That's big, Laur."

"What could be bigger than ordaining you?" she said.

"Dick says the standing committees and other diocesan bishops will never consent. I say they will or the world will heap scorn. Okay, I'm naive, but this is really revolutionary. Jesus would love this. Of course they killed him, but . . ."

"The church kills everything good," Laurie said.

"Not me, baby sister, not me! Don't rain on this parade. The Episcopal Church has done something outlandish. It's how God works, big upsets. I know God is in this."

"Yeah, like *Flashdance*. Mind telling me this woman's name?"

"Barbara Clementine Harris," I said. "Don't you love it—Clementine. I looked her up."

"You called her?"

"For godsake, no. Dick, Mr. Church Encyclopedia, found out the scoop. Also, I've been a fan of hers. She writes a kick-ass justice column, called 'A Luta Continua' for *The Witness* magazine."

"Meaning?" Laurie asked.

"It's the Episcopal Church's liberal publication," I said.

"No, I mean the *luta* thing."

"Oh, Portuguese for the struggle continues. It was a rallying cry during Mozambique's 1964 war for independence against Portuguese colonial presence. So . . ."

"The *Flashdance* thing, sexism, racism, justice, et cetera. She's a feminist," Laurie said.

"Of course. Well, I think so. Blacks call it womanist. Big into civil rights, Barbara grew up in Philly, studied journalism and urban theology at Villanova, AND got a certificate in pastoral counseling. . ."

"Oh, it's Barbara now. You building a case she's like you?"

"Of course not! Well, yes, sort of. Get this: Barbara Harris worked in PR for some oil company before she was ordained, and she read for orders."

"What's that?"

"Not graduating from a proper seminary, but her rector and bishop took her vocation seriously anyway. Reading for orders is being tutored, but not having to get an official academic degree. And the best of all: Barbara Harris was the acolyte at the ordination of the first eleven women ordained priests in Philly. After she was ordained priest she was in a parish for a short time as an interim priest, then worked as a prison chaplain, and counseled industrial corporations about public policy. Don't you get it?"

"No," Laurie said.

"Laur, she hasn't been a traditional priest. I mean not on the tenured or training track, and now she's elected a bishop?"

"You want to be a bishop now? Well I'm not supporting you there," Laurie said. "Gotta go."

"No, wait one serious damn second. I mean that not every ordained woman in the church has to follow the traditional track, like my working as a priest at BlueRidge and as a pastoral counselor. Barbara Harris as bishop will look more traditional of course and she will take on executive leadership responsibilities, as well as other things she's done."

"So?" Laurie said.

"So what I'm getting at is, maybe it doesn't matter whether my ministry as a priest is in a parish. Maybe I don't have to feel guilty. And I'm so damn proud of our church."

"Okay, Flashdance, bye."

After considerable political flap, as only the institutional Episcopal Church can provide, Barbara C. Harris received the necessary consents. Her election was called by some "the final crisis" for the church, and of course her "irregular" educational credentials, to say nothing of her gender and race, became the subject of controversy. I heard that when the diocesan vote count was announced, one bishop's wife fainted. Nevertheless, Barbara was consecrated the first woman bishop, and I was there for the historic event at Hynes Auditorium in Boston. Dick and I were mushed into a crowd of hundreds. We couldn't see, but we heard Presiding Bishop Edmund Browning pronounce the sentence of consecration:

"Therefore Father, Make *Barbara* a bishop in your Church. Pour out upon *him* (he remembered to say *her)* the power of your princely Spirit, whom you bestowed upon your beloved Son Jesus Christ, with whom he endowed the apostles, and by whom your Church is built up in every place, to the glory and unceasing praise of your Name."

All the bishops present extended their hands to place them down on one small female head. Barbara C. Harris, priest, had just become a prince, or at least "princely," but that day I didn't care about language, any more than I did on my own hands-on day. It was all gathered in Christ, and all pronouns merged. When the new bishop stood up, we still couldn't see her, but we saw her golden pointed mitre and knew that under it was our church's first woman bishop, and a black woman to boot, saying to God, herself, and all of us present through her microphone, "Go for it!"

I relished this *point vierge* moment in which Mystery stepped in and stopped the planets. When such a thing happens you hold your breath; then you cry; then you clap your hands; then you rise to your feet; then you cheer; then you fly without wings. Or that's what I did.

There were rumors of layoff at BlueRidge. Administration (think corporate) and Clinical, though all working in the same building, had different goals, little communication, and even less mutuality. My position and many others were threatened because the business was floundering. The patient community wrote a petition, signed by each one of them, urging the CEO to keep me on as chaplain. It carried heart weight, but no business clout. As a product of the 1970s and 1980s and a recovering stay-at-home housewife I had a compulsion to hold my own financially. Dick said we didn't need the money. *I* needed the money. I was a good pastoral counselor, but what would I do if I got laid off and was left with only one paying job, not even in a parish?

My old friendly three inner voices pulled me in different directions: the sweetly mild-mannered, stolidly reasonable, and occasionally high-minded voice advised me to wait and see what God would provide; the provocative, punchy voice of dissonance prodded me to challenge the rigidity of the parochial model; and the nomadic voice, amidst and beyond at the same time, counseled exploration. What I wanted was a word from the fourth friendly presence, God. I consulted Pierre, who was now my regular spiritual director, not just on retreats.

"Lyn, you are longing for a word from the Lord," he said. "You are a lost priest. And you are *my* priest. We will do the Spiritual Exercises."

"What?"

He explained in sketchy form that the Spiritual Exercises of St. Ignatius of Loyola, founder of the Jesuits, are an intense thirty-day retreat experience during which an "exercitant" (Ignatian vocabulary) spends time in silence and prayer, visiting a trained spiritual director each day.

"But I can't go anywhere for a month," I protested.

"There is the Nineteenth Annotation, a way to follow the path of spiritual growth over the course of a year, praying at home for an hour a day, then reporting to your spiritual director every two weeks. We always start with the Principles and Foundations: you are created *by* love, you go *to* love, and every day you walk *in* love. We don't proceed into sin, walking the life of Jesus, or into his passion, until you are secure in the basics. So, we go?"

It sounded rigorous and terrifying. An hour of prayer a day? But Pierre said I would be free, free, free, swallowing his adorably French *r*'s. So, I went. This Nineteenth Annotation had the lure of the Nineteenth Amendment.

There were assigned scriptural passages for guidance and I kept a journal with two column headings: prayer life and daily life. It was amazing how often the two converged. I still have my journals from this experience, and little graphs charting my consolations (feeling at one with God, self, and neighbor) and desolations (dips in serenity to say the least.) I knew from under the table that God loved me, and therefore Jesus would likely be on my side, but I couldn't imagine immersion in the life of Jesus. Praying an hour each day meant getting up at an ungodly hour. My children didn't live at home now, but I was a working woman who needed her sleep. I fussed. Then one day I set my alarm for 5:30 a.m. and got up to pray my hour—no idea what happened to my resistance. The Exercises turned out to be the most transformative experience of my life—as a Christian and more. It's hard to say exactly how, but I think it was bonding with the Jesus of the Gospels, and realizing that so many of the trials in his life had emotional parallels to mine. And all that prayer time, during which nothing happened but everything potentiated, got me clear-hearted.

There is a point in the process, after you know you're loved and you've sinned anyway, when the retreatant chooses between two standards, Christ's and Satan's, heaven and hell. The choice was not an intellectual one. I didn't even believe in hell, but I had to follow Jesus there, just to check out my capacity to resist Satan, "the evil one" according to Ignatius. I tried to shrug off the battalion of little red devils with pitchforks that hovered over my right shoulder and stanch the flames of fear leaping in my heart. I closed my eyes and descended into hell. Later I wrote:

> *I know what Hell is. Hell is drunkenness. Hell is the coiled torture of a sleepless body. Hell is listening for every sound—house creaks, the thud of a footfall on the stairs, the muffled fury of raised voices downstairs. Hell is slamming doors. Hell is children sitting on the top stair waiting for it to be over. Hell is waking to the sudden warm splash of your father's piss on your head. Hell is a siren screaming at the night. Hell is an eight year old trying to hang himself with his own socks. Hell is being forced to kneel on uncooked rice on the kitchen floor and recite the Lord's Prayer over and over. Hell is being locked in a trunk, maybe forever. Hell is stale cigarette breath and the pungent odor of whiskey next to you in the bed. Hell is the unstoppable, sleep-breaking roar of snoring. Hell is teeth-gnashing, jaw-clenching, body-breaking aloneness. Hell is always blushing and not knowing why. Hell is life in ambush. Hell is where God is not. Hell is praying and praying and no one comes. Hell is where no love lives at all.*

The words tumbled out unbidden—experiences of BlueRidge patients, counseling clients, and a few of my own. Medieval Christian theology called this experience the Harrowing of Hell, representing the time between the crucifixion and the resurrection when Jesus entered hell to retrieve all the tortured souls for the sake of divine love. A harrow is a heavy plough-like implement with sharp tines that drag over land to remove weeds and cover seed. By God, when your soul is raked over, it hurts like hell. I shivered and wrapped a blanket around me as I sat in my prayer chair. I decided I'd better write about heaven too, since Jesus obviously had to be in both of these non-places, the non-places we experience all our lives. I wrote:

Heaven is your little sister's hand reaching for yours under the covers. Heaven is a teacher who smiles and tells you you're smart. Heaven is the tiny star so far away but bright outside the window. Heaven is the sun coming every day without fail and the moon over us at night. Heaven is that you can pray. Heaven is that you have been in the slaughterhouse and you're not slaughtered. Heaven is that you have been in Hell and you heard in a creed that Jesus had been there too.

It struck me as ironic that the structures and prayer assignments I dutifully followed to the letter but first judged as uptight/rigid were exactly what made it safe enough for my imagination to take flight into the realm of Spirit—to be free. Did I get my "word from the Lord" as promised? Not exactly, but I have never again thought of Jesus as some faraway ethereal ghost, in heaven or hell.

CHAPTER 13 Flat Tire in the Snow

My fears about the BlueRidge layoffs came true. The bottom line ruled. The BlueRidge ministry was my "baby." Having it eliminated felt like an "abortion." I felt erased, as if I'd arrived at a familiar place and suddenly no one had ever heard of me. It broke my heart to leave my first beloved parish/non-parish.

More important than money and even grief was the question of how and where I could be a priest without a parish, even a "fake parish." Priests at clergy gatherings introduced themselves as rector, curate, assistant at St. Whoever. I wanted to be able to say that. Priests not full time in parishes were labeled in various ways:

- *nonstipendiary*, but we made money in various ministries;

- *non-parochial*, though most of us served in parishes in some way, even on Sundays;

- *extra-parochial*, which had a pejorative ring to it, like extramarital.

John the Baptist and Jesus, I rationalized, both eschewed the confines of institutional ministry and made Christian sainthood; Jesus got all the way to Messiah. Okay, so one got beheaded and the other crucified by the political and religious institutions of the day.

I, however, got rescued by the same institution that had twice rejected me.

"Is this Lyn Brakeman?" the female voice said at the other end of the phone.

"Yes," I said.

"This is Joan Jones, the diocesan deployment officer. I called to inquire if you'd like to be interviewed to be an interim priest at St. Mary's in Enfield. The bishop thinks you'd be great for it," she said.

"Great," I said, my heart doing a little flashdance. "I mean yes, I'd be willing to be interviewed."

"Dick, Dick, I got a parish job." I ran into the living room to tell him.

"What? But I thought . . ."

"Well, only an interview, but Joan Jones called, and the bishop thinks I'd be great in Enfield. Interim. Of course I know 'the bishop thinks you'd be great' is code for 'we need someone quick' but I don't care. Let's eat out."

"You can be so difficult," he said. "Where?"

"Some restaurant in Enfield of course."

Enfield was even farther away than Suffield. The financial package was a big bonus: my salary was based on what the former rector of thirty years, with incremental raises, had made. Flushed with affluence and prestigious hopes, I plunged in, this time with more authority and experience. I felt normal—in charge as a real interim parish priest, not an understudy. Maybe I could be a parish priest after all. I was back up to two jobs and a home, each at least forty-five minutes distant from the other two—northwest, southeast, northeast.

The St. Mary's people were warm, and I needed warming while I grieved BlueRidge. The congregation was a mix of blue- and white-collar folks, down-to-earth, pleasant. I loved altar duty, but pulpit preaching gave me gas. My preferred style of preaching remained conversational, perhaps a sign of women's relational ways and perhaps my need not to be too set apart. It's hard to chat from an elevated pulpit.

"So get outta the pulpit," Dick said.

"Would that be part of not being a little man like Madeleine instructed? I've passed the priests-shouldn't-wear-dangling-earrings test already."

"Do I look like a woman?" Dick said.

"Right. No earrings. No pulpit."

I abandoned the pulpit, which annoyed a few people, and began to preach from the crossing at center aisle. Preaching could be a pretty intimate experience, I learned. Although I did all the talking, a stream of energy came back to me from the congregation. It was like, but not quite like, the black preachers I'd heard in seminary who encouraged congregational talk back, such as "Preach it brother!" or "Glory Halleluiah!" Feedback motorized the process and taught me that even a solo wasn't solo.

God creator in Genesis wasn't as absolute as some church teaching would have us believe. In the beginning, after all, God started up a relationship with the murky muck of matter. Whatever was there mattered to

God—enough to get something going. I didn't think God wanted to be alone any more than I did. The church taught creation *ex nihilo* but I didn't buy it. "Formless and void" does not mean nothing. Matter of course got feminized while divinity/God/Spirit got masculinized—and paternalized. Yet here I was, a woman priest, the embodiment of "muck," chatting up a whole congregation—and feeling accompanied.

I wasn't a rector, though I had a parish title and was in charge, yet I felt lonely as the leader. At BlueRidge I'd worked in the company of a clinical staff in easy and regular contact—for lunch, kvetching, humor, advice, regular supervision, required for most helping professions, but not for clergy. We were a community of therapeutic leaders. In the parish I felt too executive. It wasn't just the commute that exhausted me, it was the lack of shared leadership. For instance, at St. Mary's there had been complaints about noisy children in church on Sundays. I took the problem to the vestry and we set guidelines asking parents to take better charge of disruptive children and thus respect the needs of the whole community. WE made a policy. WE put it in the bulletin. WE advertised ourselves as willing to listen to concerns about the policy. I thought it was teamwork until THEY, with few exceptions, referred upset parents to ME, and one weepy mother told me a vestry person had agreed with her that MY policy excluded children, specifically hers, from God's presence.

The *title test* was a burden as well. Some women priests by now were calling themselves Mother. Male priests called themselves Father, after God. But why perpetuate some sort of dependency with parental titles? The more generic title, Pastor, conjured images of shepherd's crooks and bleating flocks, yet some clergy referred to parishioners as their "flock." Don't become a little man, Madeleine had said. Maybe a shepherdess frolicking on the green, or Little Bo Peep? I asked people to call me Lyn (Rev., if parents thought children needed formality) and also refrained from signing my name Lyn+. The sign of the cross is meant to identify Christian clergy, but I couldn't look at it without seeing "plus sign." Bishops traditionally used it *before* their first names, and priests and deacons placed their little crosses *after* their names. I knew some women thought it was a way to be equal to the men, but I was keeping Madeleine's commandment, shedding patriarchal garb.

People argued that Jesus called God "Father." I argued back that Jesus called only fishermen as disciples, so should we all take up fishing? Are Christians to copycat behaviors or try to live by the spiritual core of the Christ nature, which is unconditional love? Jesus was remembered as calling God *Abba,* a term of affection, some thought, but historically the title originated with third-century desert ascetics, wise and holy men *and* women called *Abbas* and *Ammas.* It was a title of respect for spiritual teachers of wisdom, no one's parents. Jesus grew up. I was trying to.

Maybe I had "authority issues"—one of the church's fondest declarations about women. Of course I did. I was a woman entrenched in a patriarchy. The cute, weak, feminine object-woman remained the firm stereotype. We prayed *He* and worshiped *Him Himself* in *His* name. God was not a boy's name but before you know it, someone might risk such a naming, or be brash enough to suggest God as a choice for a boy's name in one of those books that offers a million names for the unborn holy innocents.

"How can you have been a parish priest for—how long now?" I asked Dick.

"Almost twenty-five years," he said. "You worry too much. You have authority issues."

"No kidding! But really, Dick, why do you love this so much? You pop back with an adorable perkiness, like a rubber duckie. You're unsinkable."

"At least I'm not yellow."

I tossed a yellow kitchen sponge at him. Then we sat down opposite one another at the kitchen island table, propped our chins on our fists, our elbows on the table, and looked at each other.

"You shouldn't feel badly about this," Dick said. "Parish priest was never your ministry. You only wanted to do the Eucharist, not run a small business on mostly volunteer labor and all-volunteer giving. Besides, I'm an extrovert. The cathedral where I grew up had splendor and dress-up and wonderful priests, models and mentors who treated me with respect. I used to put Dad's shirts on backwards and play priest."

"I played at it too, but I'd never seen any priests so I made one up and had communion under the table, with four invisible attendees."

"One of them divine," Dick reminded me.

"But you were a boy among men. I had no such models as a kid," I said.

As I said this I thought back to when I first saw Dick being a priest in a tiny rural parish in Maine on Labor Day weekend in 1978. He strode in, accompanied by a miniature boy acolyte carrying a huge cross, and began the liturgy in full voice with a wide grin to a congregation of ten people, five of whom were on Trinity's search committee. He treated the place as if it were a grand cathedral. That's a good priest, I thought.

"You celebrate Eucharist with integrity. That's a faithful priest," he said. "You'll make your own model."

He was right about me. I was right about him.

On reflection I realized that, except for Dick, my mentor models weren't career rectors. Neither Elmore McKee nor Madeleine L'Engle were ordained, yet both were "priests" who with authority had consecrated the best in me. Bishop Walmsley, who in his fifteen-year episcopate had ordained many women, had at first fretted, "What's the matter with you women? Why don't you want to be rectors?" In time he would fret about the numbers of women in their middle years seeking ordination—empty-nest syndrome. So what did the church want—women before kids, or after kids, or during kids? Single might spell lesbian, even more terrifying.

What really constituted priestly authority? Arthur's own career had included rectorships, yet he was a priest whose priesthood thrived for years in ministries for the national church, always with a focus on the politics of justice for the marginalized. And he'd certainly been a bishop/priest to me. My Jesuit spiritual director Pierre Wolff had left the Roman Catholic Church, his order, and his native land to marry a former nun. I'd officiated at his marriage where a Roman Catholic guest had commented with astonishment, "Look, the priest has earrings!" I'd had jitters but felt authoritative celebrating the Eucharist for a bunch of Roman Catholics. Pierre became an Episcopal priest, and continued his ministry as a spiritual director. The Rev. Lee McGee, one of the "valid but irregular" women ordained in 1975, was a college chaplain, and her principal priestly ministry was as a therapist and a teacher. And even Rector Steve, my "Gabriel," had left parish ministry to become a school chaplain.

After a year in Enfield, I felt ragged, irritable, and anxious. "I'm not man enough for this job," I told Dick, who said something stronger than baloney. I was "man" enough, I decided, but not "woman" enough.

There comes a moment in most human lives when one, despite emotional ambivalence, is gripped by a sure knowledge that one's work, even vocation, drains more of one's life energy than it replenishes. What one does to rebalance happens sometimes by chance, sometimes by decisive choice, sometimes by intervening forces from without, and sometimes by sheer grace.

For me all such forces converged on a snowy Sunday morning. My faithful Subaru began to jump and bump as it jolted forward on a flat tire. I was on a back road at least five miles south of Enfield at 7:15 a.m., and my presence was expected for the 8 a.m. service. Dick couldn't rescue me. AAA would take hours. Cell phones hadn't been invented.

The faces of the eight o'clock congregation, all twelve of them, swam through my frantic mind. I'd grown fond of this small but hardy battalion of church troopers who never missed a Sunday, but I didn't understand why small parishes continued to suffer so much heating expense, clergy time, and energy on this cost-ineffective service. My point of view was practical, but other clergy thought that the pastoral needs of even these few should be accommodated, whether it made sense or not. I knew that "these few" wanted to get their church done early, so they could all go out to breakfast for another "eucharist." There was nothing wrong with that, of course, but I felt like a martyr to the cause—also, I'd have loved to join them.

The snow thickened and my car hobbled along. Charlie would tap his watch and Mildred would scowl with flared nostrils. Evie would grin and bear it. I felt indispensable to their souls, and they to mine. I was nearing Rosemary's house—shelter in the stormy blast.

Rosemary had been a parishioner at Calvary, one of whom I'd grown fond. She'd been a lector at my ordination. Surely she would save me. Never mind that she had small children and a husband still asleep. I hammered at the door. A sleepy Rosemary opened it and woke up fast at the sight of the first woman priest she, a former Roman Catholic, had ever known, trying to be dignified and polite while telling a breathless tale of woe and stomping the snow off her boots on Rosemary's front stoop.

"No problem, I'll run you up to Enfield," Rosemary said.

She put her coat on over her bathrobe, slipped bare feet into boots, and we hopped into her Jeep. As we pulled onto the road and went a short distance, Rosemary began to laugh hysterically. She looked at me and twisted her face up. "We're out of gas. Shit. Sorry."

"How out?" I leaned over to see the gauge.

"One way to tell. There's a station in less than a mile. We'll make a run for it. Shit, I don't have my license or any money!"

"I've got money. Drive slowly," I said as if slow driving would make the gas last longer.

Two women, one in a clerical collar and the other in pajamas, made a gas run in a snowstorm, all for the love of God—or the eight o'clockers. We made it to Enfield at 7:59. I kissed Rosemary, rushed in, put on my vestments, forced myself to slow down, and entered the sanctuary, cool as a fried green cucumber, by 8:03, two minutes before Charlie usually looked at his watch.

"The Lord be with you," I said. The Lord *is* with you, I thought—and with me also.

CHAPTER 14 Who Is a Faithful Priest?

I left St. Mary's before they found their rector. I voted no to being anyone's rector, in part because of personal stress but more deeply because,
well, I discerned and took authority over my vocational direction.

The New Testament Jesus I'd met in the Exercises would make a lousy
rector. He wasn't the type—no business plan, too mobile, rushing along,
hurling God's word in people's faces, piercing the flesh of their souls with
shards of divinity—and Jewish besides. Yet I loved his mobility, his flexible,
versatile ministry. I didn't want to be tied to parochial politics and didn't
care about details like acolyte schedules. How I would be a priest would
unfold. I decided to pursue my gifts and call to be a pastoral counselor and
let God figure out the rest since a sacramental vocation was, at least in part,
HIS idea.

The Exercises taught me that the church was no more holy than other
institutions of goodwill, it just had lofty aspirations that, when repeatedly
remembered in prayer and worship, called it back to its center. It is preten-
sion to holiness that makes the church unholy. In truth we don't go TO
church, we make it.

Episcopal women priests were struggling to find a place in an institution fraught with backlash, but an institution that faithfully kept on studying women in ministry. While I recovered from my hell, I picked up some
harrowing stories from other women priests who had been ordained in
the eighties. Lee McGee, ordained "illegally" in 1975, said there was still a
double standard.

Lyn: "Because of our sex?"

Lee: "Because of our sex. Where can they fit us in?"

Lyn: "Maybe it would be easier to have an all-male priesthood, even
though it distorts the image of God. What the hell am I saying?"

Lee: "Look at what's happening to women priests even ten or more years out. Women are being placed in failing parishes. Remember Margaret's first parish? She had to preside over its closing. And you do remember that all of us women who were priested before the church voted we could be priests, received letters of inhibition?"

Lyn: "Meaning?"

Lee: "That we couldn't practice as priests."

Lyn "So what did you do?"

Lee: "While we waited for regularization. Dumbarton Oaks, a United Methodist Church in D.C., offered a space for us to celebrate Holy Eucharist. Dumbarton was the first racially mixed congregation in the 1800s. They opened the door to us Episcopal outcasts on the basis of remembering how blacks, too, had been excluded, and their own debt to the civil rights movement."

Lyn: "Wow! You had something our group of innocents didn't have, Lee. You had each other."

Lee: "Can you believe I wrote a letter to the Philadelphia women asking them to wait, not to do anything to jeopardize church unity or risk schism?"

Lyn: "No!"

Lee: "I changed my mind, of course."

Lyn: "How come?"

Lee: "I was a deacon strongly called to be a priest. At the core of it my vocation has to do with my own disability [Lee is legally blind] and wanting to align myself with people who were seen as "unfit" in the church. Why collude with domination politics?"

Lyn: "Getting excluded on the basis of gender alone, also a disability."

Lee: "Want to know the irony of it all?"

Lyn: "Are you kidding? Go. I'm woefully ignorant about all this history."

Lee: "Well, the kerfuffle about women's ordination had less to do with women than with men."

Lyn: "How so?"

Lee: "Lots of men were in favor of women as priests. The vote to ordain women, though, was quickly and officially labeled 'a breach of collegiality' in the all-male House of Bishops as it struggled to adjust."

Lyn: "Men betraying men, patriarchal ways?"

Lee: "For the most part, yes."

Lyn: "Jesus H. Christ, as my dad would say."

All I could envision were comic strips picturing boys setting up a "secret" tree house club with huge signs that read "NO GIRLS ALLOWED." Such a threatening mystery we women are. Thank God for the bishops who stepped down and out of their "tree houses" to ordain the women outside of canon law. Of course they were retired and less vulnerable than the seated bishops, but without such courageous partnerships, women would have had to wait forever for the old institution to take down its NO ADMITTANCE signs.

As I looked back at how isolated I'd felt, I envied Lee's community of women deacons-in-waiting. They'd met and prayed regularly together as they debated breaking into the institution. They organized to break the law, like the civil rights activists did. Still, any number of fierce things can also happen when action is taken in *compliance* with a new law if that law upends long-held prejudices that touch humanity's core fears—little things like sex and race.

After the Rt. Rev. Barbara C. Harris had started her Episcopal ministry in Massachusetts, she received vile hate mail and death threats for years. A good friend escorted her home every night. This small black woman "first," with a golden mitre on her head, had too much authority for comfort and precipitated discomfort. What must it have felt like to be the one woman in the House of Bishops? Being a minority of one can feel worse than being valid but irregular in a group. I'd have felt some combination of panic and jaunty bravado. Many bishops were welcoming of course. The fifteenth bishop of Massachusetts, the late M. Thomas Shaw, consecrated in 1995, gave Barbara the place of honor due her office and her person. Still, shunning continued to make a travesty of gospel hospitality for years.

My good heart appreciated the emotional authenticity of patriarchal shame and grief at the loss of long-cherished values, privileges, and power, but mostly I hated the fact that we women were its object. Barbara Harris's chutzpah assured both her popularity and her election. She refused to wear a bulletproof vest the day of her consecration because such contraptions didn't do much for a woman's physique. And on her first visitation to a parish when a parishioner wondered if she should kiss her ring, Barbara replied, "Forget the ring, honey, and kiss the bishop." She had a difficult time trying to teach a bunch of eager but unrehearsed monks, one of them the diocesan bishop, to do the electric slide. Barbara was a "steel magnolia" transported north.

"To become the first woman bishop," she wrote to me, "was a heavy responsibility in many ways. The work of the office in and of itself is difficult, but the added weight of knowing that you are an icon to some and an iconoclast to others makes life burdensome. The prayerful support of so many people made it bearable and often pleasant." *Pleasant*, a carefully muffled word.

Joan Horwitt, who started in the ordination process when I did, and was the first woman to be ordained priest in Connecticut, told me, with brilliant wit and scorn, that she hadn't been a priest for very long before she attended an ordination with her rector and boss. On arrival they went to the room where gathered clergy vested. She was stopped at the door by a laywoman, who said, "Oh dear, what are we going to do with *you?*" *Will an empty broom closet do?* Joan thought, and went to vest in the women's bathroom. Another woman priest at a liturgical event was told she couldn't vest with the men. She'd draped her vestments over her arm, latched onto her rector's arm, and said breezily, "Oh, it's okay, we get dressed together every Sunday morning." Do people think we clergy take off our clothes to vest? You'd think the sacristy was a strip club. Laughter kept women alive and well enough to be fruitful in various ministries.

"What is it you do now, dear?" my mother asked.

"I'm a priest, Mom."

"But you're not in a parish."

"I know, but I'm becoming a good pastoral counselor. There are lots of priest counselors," I said, knowing I sounded defensive. She was right that I didn't look usual.

"Oh, good, dear," she smiled. "I'm sure I'll see you being a priest some time."

Mom didn't care much for Jesus, and the weekly Eucharist was a ritual she didn't wax enthusiastic about. I couldn't explain to her that in my counseling vocation I was being true to the zeal I'd had since childhood for probing the depths of psyche and soul for spiritual truth—a penchant so outside my mother's repertoire that she used to shake her head at me and say, "Why can't you just take things at face value?" I was clearly a hopeless case in her book, but if I'd followed her advice—"Oh darling, just be happy no matter what!"—I'd still be feeling inadequate and puzzling over Norman Vincent Peale's *Power of Positive Thinking*, a book she gave me when I was in seventh grade. Nancy Drew and the Bible—both containing strong women leaders—had been more page-turning than Peale. As a kid I'd hated happiness and practiced the big sulk, but just in case I really was happiness deficient I'd read Peale, then told my mother it was "bullshit," to which she'd airily replied, "Why, darling? I think it's the way to live."

I didn't trust my mother's über-happiness or Peale's recipe. Both felt like fake mind control. Peale I threw out, but you don't throw a whole mother away.

Annoying as my mother's query about my vocation was, it made me think. Was the Eucharist a face value celebration? Hardly, though I had to admit it was the only dining room table I knew of where no one could slap their napkin down and leave in a huff of angry tears. "I was the one daughter-in-law who never left the Gillespie family table in tears," Mom had proudly told me. I knew the tears had been shed over Dad's mother's put-down of daughters-in-law, none of them good enough. I can't say what the face value of the Eucharist would be. I just know the table is set, ready, and waiting, day after day.

When I was a new priest I felt very proud of the white collar I'd lusted after, wanting everyone to notice. Mom had thought I looked "stunning, darling." You could hardly blame me my snatch of ego, though I didn't wear my official garb in my counseling office. I would have set myself apart and pastoral counseling is about being *with*. Dick had told me that he used to act in authoritarian ways when he started out.

"Those were my Rasputin days," he said. "Even grew a beard."

"I wouldn't have loved you back then," I said.

"Probably not," he said. "But you do now. I know you worry about not having an official parish. You can celebrate at Trinity sometimes."

"Yeah, maybe, thanks," I said, unsure why I felt squeamish about that idea.

Whether I needed it or not, I wanted a parish of my own where I could celebrate Eucharist. Maybe not becoming "a little man" meant not being tolerated simply because I was Dick's wife, and maybe it also meant that priesthood had many variations. I wanted to feel God inside and out like I had under the table. I also wanted to wear my vocational authority not as armor, yet in a traditional setting. I felt most like a priest at the altar celebrating the Eucharist in a small informal group at a retreat, or in the Education for Ministry seminar I mentored, or at a parish Sunday mass.

An idea took shape: I could *volunteer* as a priest. Given Dick's and my moral slippage and my not wanting to be wifey, volunteering at Trinity wouldn't work. So I went parish shopping again and in time made a proposal to the rector of a parish not far from my home. "I'd like to be a volunteer Sunday priest in your parish, if you'll have me."

"I never heard of that," he said.

I'd never heard of it either, but I told him about my early supplemental priesthood vision, thinking now of myself, outside the parochial system but serving on Sundays—a liturgical priest.

"That's it! Worker priest. I've heard about that model, tried in the Catholic Church, right? Priests did hands-on pastoral work among dock workers. It worked until their bishops balked. Not enough control I guess," he laughed.

"Our bishops, I've heard, aren't all that happy ordaining maverick priests who want to be chaplains, counselors, et cetera, not full time in parishes. But doesn't the church need to turn itself inside out?" I said, then worried I'd gone too far with some kind of radical idea. "I make money at counseling. But I want a place to be a priest—an altar, a pulpit, and a community where I can serve every Sunday and help out when you're not there."

He smiled. "I don't mind help in getting the parish used to women priests." This priest had been a bit irregular himself, having been through treatment for alcoholism while he was the rector and then returned to the parish sober—and to keep up his recovery. This priest had been through hell and survived.

"We could call you Priest Associate, and you could be here each Sunday to celebrate at one of the two services. How about preaching?"

"Once a month. I have a day job. Oh, and could I use the church to start a Spirituality Mass for recovering people in twelve-step programs on Sunday evenings, once a month? Recovery meetings often happen in parish basements, but I've always wanted to connect the upstairs and the downstairs."

"That would be fine." He grinned and gave me keys.

I began my Sunday Priest Associate ministry and also presided at the Spirituality Mass there for six years. At first I shared the preaching ministry with a deacon who served at a neighboring parish. She was the nurse at BlueRidge who had inadvertently landed me the job when I'd told my interviewers that my Jesus had more dirt under his fingernails than hers did. We parted company with no hard feelings.

People formerly invisible in parishes, trying to recover from church, God, and alcoholism, showed up. For this small, faithful congregation I instituted the sacrament of laying on of hands for healing occasionally and felt like a priest healing my own wounds and some of theirs with words of acceptance and the sacramental meal open to all without condition. The parish rector didn't attend, so I was the priest in charge of this Spirituality Mass.

I was happy to be a Sunday Priest Associate. I had no paycheck but felt free. Without fear I pounded away at inclusive language, never called God *He* unless I had to, and tried some homiletic stunts, such as using a song from the movie *Thelma and Louise* to illustrate incarnational intimacy. And once I said that one didn't have to be a Christian to be a christ. The male parish warden thought I was prophetic; the female warden was furious and one Sunday I spotted her wagging her finger and cursing at the boom box I'd placed on a pew chair up front. I'm sure the rector fielded complaints, but he smoothed feathers and gave me my wings. I told Mom I was "normal" but she never came to see me normal.

If I had any remaining doubts as to my authenticity or efficacy as a priest, Irene dispelled them. Irene had been a BlueRidge colleague. She came for counsel about an abortion she'd had years back. We talked about leftover guilt and grief, and she cried, but it seemed something more was needed.

"Do you have any sense what sex your child would have been?" I asked.

"Yes. A boy. I'm sure," she said.

"Did you give him a name?" I asked.

"Jeffery. He'd be fifteen by now," she answered.

"Is there something you want Jeffery to know?" I asked. "Or to know from him?"

Irene wrote letters to her son. The practice helped. But I had another idea.

"I'm a priest," I said. "Do you think you'd like your son baptized?"

We sat together in quietness. She held the invisible ghost of the son she'd named Jeffery in her cupped hands and gave him a middle name from her family. I poured some water into a Pyrex bowl we got from the kitchen, consecrated the water using prayers from the baptismal rite, and dipped my fingers into the water to baptize Irene's hands, empty but only to our eyes.

Irene thanked me for being the church for her, the church she was too ashamed to go to. In that moment and others like it, I knew my office was a sanctuary, a parish of two or three, and I was a real priest in it.

CHAPTER 15 Who Is a
Faithful Woman?

D ick had been the rector at Trinity for almost fifteen years. He wondered if we could be a rector couple. I'd ruled out rector, yet being a team rector was enticing. What if . . .

Couples serving together in parishes often ended up divorced and set up a model in which a parish didn't pay for two full-time clergy positions but got the work of two full-time priests anyway. Guess who overworked? There was a better way to do it, we thought. We wrote our vision of shared rectorship, emphasizing the value of having the full image of God (male and female) visibly present in Word and Sacrament. He had more parish experience, but I had professional pastoral counseling skills, besides specialities in addictions and the dynamics of trauma recovery—all issues that troubled parishes more than the church was, or is, willing to admit. We thought we could be a strong team. We interviewed in two Connecticut parishes and learned a lot about how people had manipulated their own parents.

One man asked at an interview: "What if, on Monday, Lyn says it's okay to do such and such, and on Tuesday Dick says it's not okay?"

"We *talk* to each other," I said. "And we'd trust each other with small decisions."

"We have mutuality in our marriage," Dick added.

"We are pleased to propose Rev. Simeone for the position as our next rector, and his wife to be his assistant rector," read the letter from the search committee. Not even my name.

He rector, *she* assistant. They weren't ready for shared authority, and we weren't ready to abandon our model, so we declined and stayed put.

I joined the Episcopal Women's Caucus to keep up with church politics. Not all diocesan bishops would ordain women or receive them into parishes in their dioceses. They were granted a conscience clause that gave them the right to refuse women. Single male consciences apparently were more important than the consciences of many. The Episcopal Church kept on studying women. Things were improving, but there was still a gender pay gap, and some of the same issues that I had faced over ten years ago, when I fought to get ordained, were still present:

- the marriage penalty (more bias against women who were married than men who were married)

- mobility (men assumed to be more geographically mobile than women)

- the balance of mothering and career—the old "dual vocation" prejudice lurking still. Women were simply clothed in the wrong gender for this institution.

But so was God, in my un-humble opinion, well, not exactly the wrong gender, but any gender at all. I was beginning to wonder about God abuse. Was it possible to abuse divinity? The church palavered about social justice for humanity all the time. What about the language that confined and defined God? I'd become quite nauseated with "*Almighty* God" this and "*Almighty* God" that. Love of course can be "almighty" in its own dear ways, but that is NOT what was meant.

My conscience was feeling offended, not just by how women were second bested, but about the disfigurement of God's image. How could we keep on masculinizing God and at the same time insist that women were fully included *and* could weekly celebrate a meal of justice and intimacy and hospitality in *HIS* name? Language to some seemed a minor issue, window dressing only. But language itself is an agent of transformation and God mediates grace as much through language as through any other powerful symbol. Still, time-honored phrasing gets into your bones and it's hard to change, even if it's no longer useful.

I'd matured enough to know that God was never a boy's name, or a girl's name either. Abstractions like Presence, Light, or even Love felt evasive. They are descriptors, not names. I needed a name! In Scripture naming is something God does, and when God recognizes a particular gift and vocation in someone, that person might get a brand-new name. Monastics take on saints' names, and sometimes people change their names (I don't mean just by marriage) as a way to signal their transformation. *Godde*, an Old English spelling some feminists were using, sounded soft and open to me, admissive of full masculinity and full femininity—a gentle reminder that we do not know and never shall what all Godde/God is about, though we get hints and glimpses. Few would argue with the idea that God is neither male nor female, but I wanted to say it not by negation: God is fully both, and everything in between.

Jesus of Nazareth presented a problem, being, without doubt, a man, but was Christ a man? In prayer I'd experienced Jesus as remarkably non-sexist, sexy maybe, but not owned by his maleness. Okay, he picked men as disciples, but really, wouldn't it have been plain dumb in his historical context to try to establish a heavenly kingdom with women at the helm? The Bible stories are confusing but not insane, though maybe a tad unconventional, because women were strongly present—never written out of holy writ. For myself, Jesus being a man had been important for the healing of my relationships with men. It was precisely because Jesus was a human man who loved in such a remarkable way that I knew him to be divine. Paradoxically, the more I let go of my worry about the proportions of divinity and humanity in Jesus, the more divine he became, deserving of his messianic title, the Christ, the anointed one, a title that transcended Jesus' gender. So why masculinize Christ? *All* Christians are *in* Christ, the body of Christ. But who thinks of a woman when we say *he?* I didn't want to emasculate Jesus or make God a woman; nor did I want to italicize pronouns. I wanted to eliminate them, along with the domination of the Father metaphor—for Christ's sake.

As a liturgical priest, when I elevated the bread and wine to praise God for such a graciously humble mystery, I longed but did not dare to say, "By Christ, and with Christ, and in Christ, in the unity of the Holy Spirit, all honor and glory is yours, Almighty God [sic], now and for ever." Oh, that sounded so much better than "by him and with him and in him" and "Almighty Father," and oh, it sounded so "meet and right" to my craving soul.

Godde being all feminine and all masculine—and everything in between—clear and discrete, not all mushed up in an androgynous spiritual blend—I fell quickly, madly, and secretly in love with this notion. I was becoming a zealot, full of hubris, thinking I could defend God for godsake. Really! Godde probably didn't give two figs about pronoun politics, but I couldn't shut up: masculinized power language was hurting women and others who felt excluded and unfairly ejected from almighty Love. Why not start another vocation? Committee One had worried that I couldn't handle two, but I'd already had five (cocktail hour survivor, mother, priest, counselor, spiritual director)!

I went to a writers weekend led by Madeleine L'Engle. She introduced the first session by saying: "Pick someone in Scripture who you think might be angry and write about it." Immediately, and with sly irony, the snake in Genesis slithered into my mind. Imagine being scapegoated for the whole messy Eden affair, known dramatically by Christians as the fall—a little snake causing all that sin and death? Outrageous. As my writing developed, an aging female snake had a long overdue hissy fit before her maker—who listened! The story, and others with it, became a published book entitled *Spiritual Lemons: Biblical Women, Irreverent Laughter and Righteous Rage.* It contained midrashic stories about biblical women who prayed, in impious ways like me, and found blessing. Vocation six: author.

Becoming a professional listener had made me, according to Dick, a professional talker at home. Now writing at least kept me quiet.

ᚼ

"So I'm all set in my vocation and personal life. There's nothing left to pray about," I joked with my retreat director at Mercy Center where I'd gone for my annual retreat week. It was a dangerous joke.

"Why don't you pray about alcohol? You've mentioned it on and off. Do you pray about it?" she asked.

"Oh, that issue is settled. It's not what's on my mind now," I said, irked that she had put in on my mind, and knew me well enough to do that.

"Okay," she said.

So, I was on my own then. I got right to work, spent the first day laying before God a long list of inconsequential baloney, working my way slowly down into the recesses of those dark places many imagine that Godde can't see. Perhaps for some people deep prayer is a highway to heaven and enlightenment, but for me it was usually more like a strip search of my soul. Mystical traditions called this process self-emptying, in Greek *kenosis.* Paul preached that Christ emptied *himself* to become fully human—as divine and human he would neither compromise nor exploit either nature. Such humility brought exaltation. Well, well, by that standard all women ought to be automatically exalted for self-emptying.

Well, I didn't care about following Christ into exaltation. I just wasn't up to that much required humility. It had taken me years to fill myself up

137

with my own feminine pride and worth and agenda. I wasn't about to let myself be emptied. But Paul, as was his wont, had more to say, and for me the "more" was, save one pronoun that needed italics, what I needed to hear: "Therefore, my beloved . . . work out your own salvation with fear and trembling; for it is God who is at work in you, enabling you both to will and to work for *his* good pleasure" (Phil. 2:12ff). The letter ends with final instructions not to worry but to let anything and everything be known to God. So I did.

Godde, I don't want to be empty, I want to be full of you—and me.

"I don't know what to pray," I said the next day to my director, avoiding the emptying issue.

"Try the *Suscipe*," she suggested.

The *Suscipe* is an old saw of a prayer, attributed to St. Ignatius of Loyola, whom I knew well by now. While laid up healing from a bad wound, Ignatius read about the life of Jesus and redirected his life from its attachment to wealth and nobility to a spiritual attachment to Christ, whom he strove to imitate. He prayed: *Take, Lord, and receive all my liberty, my memory, my understanding and my entire will, all I have and call my own. You have given all to me, to you, Lord, I return it. Everything is yours; do with it what you will. Give me only your love and your grace, that is enough for me.* His body healed but his soul was never the same.

Radical emptying. All that day I suscipe'ed with vigor and failed. I couldn't let go because damned alcohol demanded attention. I was unsure where to place myself on the continuum from self-righteous teetotaler to constant drunk. In my family we had both ends and the whole range of middling variations. I'd never prayed about my own alcohol use, only that of others. The lovely *Suscipe* didn't grip me—too much God, not enough room for me.

"Try the *Anima Christi*," my director suggested on the third day. Another Ignatian favorite, this one highlighted intimacy and was not so pushy about surrender.

Soul of Christ sanctify me.
Body of Christ save me.
Blood of Christ inebriate me.
Water from the side of Christ wash me.
Passion of Christ strengthen me.

O good Jesu, hear me.
Within thy wounds hide me.
Suffer me not to be separated from thee.
From the malignant enemy defend me.
At the hour of my death call me
and bid me come to thee
that with thy saints I may praise thee
for ever and ever. Amen.

I'd prayed this when I did the Spiritual Exercises, but now it got to me. I felt partnered in the flesh—and even *inebriated* at the thought of such bonding—better than alcohol. I sat still in the chapel and recited the *Anima* over and over, silently and aloud.

"So you felt more present? Good. Time for the tomb," my good director declared the next day.
"The tomb. Why?"
"It's empty," she said.
"But I just got full," I whined.
I read the story of the empty tomb in the Gospel of John (20:1–18). Mary Magdalene, blinded by tears (my kind of woman), stooped to peer in, looking for her beloved Jesus. I envisioned a cavernous dark space and peered in; my imagination was quickly seized by an image. In the tomb I saw a tiny dining room table, with a miniature family sitting around it: my parents, Laurie, and myself. I blinked to get rid of the odd image. It expanded. A large finger, seeming to approach over my right shoulder, thrust itself into the cave, tipped over the table with exquisite precision and tenderness, and beckoned me to follow. I didn't want to. I tried to get Laurie to come with me, but she was completely ensconced. So I left, riding the finger of God like Thumbelina.

"Lyn, it's a vision. Stay with it. It's telling you something," my director said the next day, leaning over and nearly falling off her chair. Her intense reaction scared me, but not away.
Jesus left the tomb. So could I. I began to direct my prayers to Jesus. In truth he seemed more manageable than God as Almighty and Father, easy to unload on, obsess with, nag, bawl in front of, and wrestle with. What was

leaving like for him? Was it like leaving home, leaving what? The rest of the day I walked around with prayer burning in my heart and possessing my mind like an annoying tune: *Where are you, Jesus? And what do you have to say to me? Oh, I know the end of the story, you're in heaven, and hell too, but really where are you and what happened?*

That night I wrapped myself in a blanket my son John had given me, and in my nightgown and socks padded to the cold, dimly lit chapel to pray. I sat on a cushion and turned my gaze to the floor-to-ceiling oil painting of a rose, multi-petaled, majestic, standing alone on a long green stem, thorns along each side. I scarcely noticed the faint background cross that shadowed the bright rose. The rose was profuse, ample enough to enfold and soft enough to comfort. I stayed there for what seemed like my lifetime. A shiver brought me back to the chapel, its cold creeping into my bones, and I left to go back to my warm room and bed.

Through a deep sleep, the word *straddling* came to me. It woke me so I got up and looked out my window: No moon. No stars. No light anywhere in the complex. I turned on my light, wrapped myself in my blanket, and opened my journal.

"Suffer me not to be separated from you." I wrote the line from the *Anima* that had adhered to my soul.

Do you think I can drink safely or not, Jesus?

The next day my spiritual director, of course, thought God, Jesus too, was saying something, inviting something.

"God wants straddling? Aren't we supposed to come down on one side or the other? Isn't that the biblical idea? No wishy-washy?" I said.

She shrugged.

I went to the dictionary. *Straddle*: It means all kinds of things, including equivocation, but the definition that struck me was "sit or stand with legs far apart, one leg on either side of." All I thought of was sex, gynecological exams, rodeo cowboys, and Anglicans straddled between Catholic and Protestant. I spent that day wondering. I could be a straddler—not a rodeo cowboy on a fierce hurtling bull, not a woman in stirrups waiting for some doctor to probe her vagina, not a woman spreading her legs to admit a penis, and not an indecisive woman lacking purpose. I was straddled about alcohol, trying to keep a balance between getting drunk and abstinence. Again that night I awoke before dawn's light and felt the impulse to write. I wrote until I saw the shadows of the night lift.

My mother didn't drink at all until she was forty. Why did she start? Curiosity about my mom had been my constant companion, and no less now.

Once, I'd interviewed her, for a graduate course I took.

"Any regrets, Mom?" I asked.

"I regret I couldn't make it work to be part of Bill Brakeman's life after you two divorced."

"But Mom, Bill is remarried."

"I know he's remarried, dummy. I gave them a set of luggage for their honeymoon. And then I wasn't even invited to their first wedding anniversary party."

"But why would they invite you?" I asked.

"Lynnie," she said looking straight at me, "I adored Bill Brakeman. I thought he was just right for you and when it didn't work I still . . ."

She didn't finish her sentence and for once I didn't ask. At that moment I knew that she had "married" Bill and I had followed, fearing, without knowing it, that my own fragile love for him could never measure up to hers. I had divorced Bill and he had found the courage to "divorce" her.

I switched topics. "What about your feelings about God or religion?" Maybe a higher power would help us cry together.

"Oh, I love God. I'm not sure about religion, but . . . no offense to you, darling."

"I'm not offended," I said. "I have doubt too."

"I don't doubt God, of course," she said. "I still have that Russian icon my daddy brought me from his travels when I was a child. I'd kiss it every night." I waited. Her gaze drifted off. "When I die," she continued, "I will go to heaven and put my head in God's lap, and everything will be all right." She looked over at me and smiled, a far-off smile. We were silent together.

Later she gave me the icon, a sliver of her spirituality. The icon's frame was tarnished and the painted icon insertions of Christ's face and hands in the classic position of giving a blessing were missing. I took it to a Russian Orthodox priest in Hartford to ask what it meant. It was my way of honoring the mystery of my mom.

The priest polished the tarnished silver framing and told me it was Christ Pantokrator, meaning Christ of all Potency or Power. He spoke placidly about the sovereignty of Christ—no ambiguity. I stood listening and watching and feeling a little envy, my faith being the wrestle-to-the-mat kind. His Christology leaned more toward the divine side of Christ's nature than mine, but his faith shone as he talked and cut, with swift deft turns of the scissor, a paper image of Christ's hands and face to insert behind the silver. He knew what he was doing as if he did this every day on an assembly line. I still have the icon.

Mom never talked of Jesus much, only God, so I had once asked her if she believed in Christ. "Of course, dummy," she'd said. I guessed Mom hated the crucifixion images—too Catholic. She hated pain and had survived plenty of it. I have a crucifix on my home altar. It's not the part of Jesus' life I dwell on but it serves as a reminder of gross injustice. It is not the last Christian word.

After my father died, Mom used wine to ease the pain of her own emptiness and her osteoporotic spine. One evening she fell going from the chaise to her bedroom. We took her to the hospital in the wee hours. Coming home, I moved ahead to get the door open and heard her weak, almost childlike, voice call out, "I'm going."

"Where?" I called back.

"I'm going," she repeated till I got it. I cleaned her up and put her to bed. It was a tender reversal; both of us hated it and both of us accepted it. For her safety, or ours, we had to limit her wine. She didn't argue, complain, or sneak. (Relinquishing her car was another story.)

I had lived in the valley of the shadow of alcohol all my life. Laurie had chosen one end of the family continuum. My father had become dependent on alcohol, medicine, I now think, to relieve the soft silent interior ache of shyness. I think the same about Bill. My mother and I had tried it all. We drank with our men for love and companionship. We drank with each other for the same reasons. We drank alone out of loneliness, and felt more lonely. I was my mother's kind of drinker, a nonalcoholic straddler.

On the last day of the retreat my spiritual director listened to my straddling story as if it were a confession. She absolved me by listening with compassion as I talked about my drinking and my mother. Then she put her hands on my head and prayed, thanking Jesus, the out-of-the-tomb one—emergent Christ.

"Where do you think you and God will go from here?" she asked.

"I don't know."

As a child I'd made a vow to prove there was nothing wrong with me. I'd made and broken one set of marriage vows, then made the same solemn vows at my second marriage. I'd made sacred ordination vows. Soon I vowed to be a straddler: I would drink without getting drunk, and if I could not do that, I would not drink at all.

I changed the phrasing of the *Suscipe*, which, along with the *Anima*, I pray daily.

Take Lord receive, my entire liberty, my will, my memory, my under-standing. All that I have you have given me. Bless and increase me and return myself to me, that I may love and serve you a hundred thousand million fold. Amen.

It's a kind of vow.

CHAPTER 16 I Thought He Was Dead

Just when you think your life is about as rich and full as it can be, something inevitably upsets that idolatrous self-satisfaction—and provides
an unexpected challenge.

For us it was a phone call from a priest in Massachusetts whom we
got to know when he ran for bishop in Connecticut. Connecticut elected
from within, as it had for centuries. It fit its image as the premier diocese,
that is, the first diocese in the American church to elect a bishop and suc-
cessfully get him consecrated. Historically, the Church of England required
an oath of allegiance to the English crown, so Samuel Seabury appealed to
Scotland, where nonjurored clergymen who had refused to take the loyalty
oath to the crown consecrated Seabury in the Church of Scotland in 1784.
It took 225 years for Connecticut to soften the cement-footed pride of its
history and elect in 2009 a bishop from outside its own diocese, a priest
from Massachusetts in fact.

The spirit of Connecticut was in our bones, so when this Massachusetts priest urged Dick to apply for the rector's position at St. John's parish
in Gloucester, Massachusetts, Dick declined. I was relieved. The Massachusetts priest continued to nag, saying "They need you." Dick agreed to
send his materials to Gloucester to make the guy shut up. We forgot about
it, until the call came requesting an interview and an onsite visit. I hoped
they wouldn't like him. Only later did we find out that this nag of a priest's
warden was the search consultant in Gloucester and had persuaded them
that they couldn't throw Dick's resumé in the slush pile, as they'd intended,
because he was "too old." The consultant said, "That's ageism."

The Gloucester search committee asked an odd question: "If you come
to St. John's how long will you stay?" Their two former priests had short ten-
ures. "I'm a stayer. Besides, where would I go? I'm fifty-five," Dick laughed.

They laughed—an endearing moment and I think a healing one, given their ageist concerns. I didn't think of my own history or healing—right then.

We moved to Gloucester in January 1997 to begin a new parochial tenure for Dick and to establish a new arena for me as a priest to assert my own Goddely agenda. It took a little persuading to convince the St. John's vestry that I could be a non-stipendiary Sunday Priest Associate. I reassured them that I would *not* be the rector, *not* share authority, would establish my own counseling practice, *not* expect any money, and further that it would be a good model to see both genders represented at the altar, the fullness of the image of God. I left pronouns and any mention of feminism out, by the grace of Godde *Herself.*

Before we left I said goodbye to Mom and asked her how she felt. "Sad," she said. No tears, but that word was the equivalent. When I was ordained Mom gave me a small framed poster she'd ordered from a catalogue. It was calligraphed in rainbow colors: "God danced the day you were born." It was the corniest, most beautiful gift I've ever received. I don't know what God did, but I knew that Mom danced the day I was born.

Leaving Connecticut and all my four children, including my brand-new first grandchild, Gillian, born in 1996, was wrenching. I felt an aching sorrow that subsided, but never really vanished. In fact, every time one of my children left after a visit, I cheerily waved and blew goodbye kisses, then sobbed as soon as they pulled away. What was wrong with me? Families do this all the time. I missed them and the easy proximity—and something more. My daughter Jill said I'd "abandoned" them. A friend expressed horror at such unreasonableness, but I knew it was emotionally plumb given our history. I had broken what had tacitly become a family rule and role: home is where the mother is. This mother moved.

Then a back story jumped up and bit us. The Gloucester parish had come under the strong influence of conservative evangelical Christians, refugees from a neighboring parish where a split over a rector and certain theological ideas had occurred. When the search committee spoke of their "theological" diversity we wondered what that meant. We found out fast, as angry men paid calls to the new rector. One said, "I don't give a damn about your theology." Another had a tantrum about progressive ideas, and still another was overheard ranting after a Sunday service, "Is he even *allowed* to preach from the Old Testament?"

A man confronted me one Sunday, saying, "Do you believe Jesus was divine?"

"Of course I do. Do you think I'd be praying to just any old guy?" I said. I felt assaulted, but such militant Christian vigor firmed up my conviction that the inclusivity and expansive love of Divinity needed a boost, and perhaps a wee bit of emasculation.

Blessed were the few who spoke up to inform Dick of the underlying tensions. One dear woman, chair of the search committee, said, "I'm not sure the committee was conscious of this, but deep down I think we knew we didn't want this direction for Gloucester." Eventually, the unhappy and the glum migrated back to the parish they'd left. A new rector had been elected there, one who had a bully pulpit for every kind of heaven-and-hell judgmentalism imaginable, all in the name of God. He was a sheep vs. goats guy—in sheep's clothing, of course.

Gloucester had beautiful ocean scenery and vast soft beaches. It also had all the problems of any urban community: drugs, alcohol, domestic violence, and difficult politics related to the slow diminishment of the fishing industry—the city's economy depended on it. I joined in the efforts of the city's Coalition for the Prevention of Domestic Abuse.

Dick and I hung in and found many like-minded friends and a parish community with pizazz and heart. We did some teaching—even worked on pronouns! It helped that the rector shared my passions—and my bed. Yes, you can use the divine name instead of *he* in most cases. You could use *Christ* instead of *he* when the Risen Lord was meant. Christ was not Jesus' last name. I made sure that anonymous and missing female voices in Scripture were acknowledged, and one woman thanked me.

I met a woman pastoral counselor, and together we established a private practice, Cape Ann Pastoral Counseling Services, with free office space in a local Congregational church. Some parishioners wondered if they got free counseling in return for free space—and whether we business "partners" by chance were lesbians? No, on both counts, but we were grateful for the small office, and established a sliding scale fee that fit our identity as pastoral counselors. I made less money than I had in Connecticut, but I soon felt abundant again, as a Priest Associate and a Pastoral Counselor.

In this new diocese, I collided with my Connecticut history in unexpected ways—one liberating, the other terrifying.

Liberating

At a special convention in the Episcopal cathedral in Boston the diocesan bishop made a pitch for annual bishops' awards to be given to laypeople who'd made significant contributions to ministry in the diocese—and I spoke publicly against it. Connecticut had an awards tradition, and I remembered the politics of pain (why him, not me?), the scoffing (she got it just for retiring at last), and the belittling (this is a token because his father is clergy). In front of hundreds of clergy and laypeople and bishops, I was scarcely aware of taking the mike as I said, "I'd like to speak against bishops' awards. Every faithful Christian in this diocese I'm sure is laboring in the vineyard with all her or his might. Special awards seem very cultural, but not very gospel."

After I spoke, Dick told me he heard people saying, "Who was that woman?" Later a few priests thanked me for saying the obvious. A bit stunned, I suddenly realized that something had lifted from my shoulders—my history. In Massachusetts I had no rejections in the ordination process, no sexual sins, real or imagined, and no shame. I was free—until another convention.

Terrifying

He's not dead yet. He is alive. He is standing on the steps of the cathedral, talking, laughing. He is short, rounded, his hair thinning and graying. I turn away, scurry to the women's room and slither into a stall. I bolt the door, sit down, put my head in my hands. I hear women coming and going. I hear them talking about the church, their families, children, parish budgets. They laugh. I stay very quiet in my stall. Only God and I can hear me think. The traffic abates. I've seen a ghost who isn't a ghost. I click my fingernail on my stiff white collar. Click and click then open the door, go to the sink, wash my hands and leave.

Back in the cathedral, I slid into the boxed pew and closed its door behind me, feeling grateful for pews with doors. I scrunched down in my seat and jammed Dick in the ribs.

"Hey, cut it out!" he said.

"Shhh. He's here."

"Who?"

"Shhh, the bishop."

"Lyn, for God's sake, the place is crawling with bishops. It's a convention."

"Shhh. Bishop Porteus. He's here. I saw him. He's alive."

"You don't keep up with church politics. He's retired and assisting here. He married an Episcopal priest of this diocese," Dick whispered.

"You should've told me. He married an Episcopal priest?"

"Shhh."

Time, I told myself as my mind wandered off on its own, was impotent, healed nothing. It had been over fifteen years since this bishop had rejected me in Connecticut. I wondered if he knew I'd been ordained. The gossip lines had buzzed about me—also gone electric about him and his divorce. I'd listened to women in my counseling office talking about love affairs with clergy, including some bishops. All these women thought it was true love and ended up swathed in shame. How come these old boys weren't taking the heat for their messes? The church set up guidelines for keeping boundaries (no touchy/feely/huggy) and invented something called "fiduciary responsibility." It sounded like a financial deal to me but it was about who had the power—the authority figure of course, the one in the collar, Father Swellington or other. *He* was responsible for holding relationships with "sheep" in trust. Therefore, no touch—or sex.

"Did you sexually harass me?" I asked Dick as I came back to real time.

"What the hell are you talking about?"

"Well, there's talk nowadays about boundaries, and clergy being the keepers thereof. So I was really innocent, right? You had all the power, and you seduced an innocent woman parishioner," I said.

"You're losing it just because you saw Porteus," he said. "Our love was consensual."

"Boy, we were lucky to slide into home base before the boundary paranoia set in. Officially you should be toast, but I was no fiduciary innocent. Do you think I should contact Porteus?"

"What for?" he said.

"Reconciliation. We preach it, no?" I said.

"Only on Sundays." He grinned.

"You're not helpful at all," I said.

"And you're too scrupulous. Do what you want. You always do anyway," he said.

"When I dare," I said, and hunched down in my seat.

The double standard Lee McGee had spoken about had put women clergy in a bind. We needed male support to realize our vocations, and most of our bosses were men, some with itchy libidos. When women began to talk, the church discovered that pastoral misconduct among male clergy was widespread and had been overlooked for centuries. When several women spoke out about a former Massachusetts bishop, he took his own life, unable, I suppose, to face public humiliation. It had been a terrible tragedy, in part the result of his personal issues, but also in part because of another cruel double standard imposed on clergy who were held to moral standards higher than the heavenly host: immune to common temptations, not expected to be in therapy, and not required to receive regular supervision as those in other helping professions did. Belated attempts to set things right in cases of pastoral misconduct often re-wounded both male clergy perpetrators who had misused the power vested in them by their office and the women who thought they were loved and were further shamed for exposing the truth.

The patriarchal institutional church resisted exposure of its sins, making a mockery of forgiveness, just as patriarchal society did. I'd been riveted to the TV during the 1991 Senate confirmation hearings for Clarence Thomas, a nominee for the Supreme Court. Anita Hill, an aide who'd worked under Thomas in two federal agencies, testified about his sexual harassment of her, and got pilloried herself. She stated that Thomas had used sexually provocative language, requested dates, and talked about watching women in pornographic films. It made her uncomfortable, but he was her boss! After she left his employ, she stepped up to testify against him during the Senate hearings. For her trouble she was called a liar, a lesbian, a sexually repressed and shameful woman. Twice shamed, once for remaining quiet and once for speaking out. (Godde knows what racist comments were included, although she and Thomas are both African American.) Hill "lost" but her testimony split the Senate. Divided, they voted to confirm Thomas by the narrowest margin ever. Anita Hill's courage put the world on notice that silence about harassment could be broken. But look who's on the Supreme Court!

For a time women were scapegoated for the "sins" of the whole system. One woman's ordination process had been halted when she was already a postulant because she fell in love and came out as a lesbian. It took years and the grace of a bishop in another diocese to finally ordain her. Another's process was stalled because she's been divorced twice and was dating one of her professors at her seminary. This "mess" had overwhelmed two bishops. Her ordination was held up for a total of twelve years, to my eleven. "It was my disastrous life that complicated it all," she told me. *Disastrous* seemed a strong, shaming word. Had she made her life that way all by herself? Would a man say this or be judged this way? With the help of Lee McGee, this postulant's file was "rescued" from the "bottom drawer." It was untidy Episcopal practice at best to keep women's files and their ordination status sequestered and unprocessed. The women who had been ordained before the vote became advocates for those of us left behind—not because of the apocalyptic rapture but by ecclesiastical sloth. Many believed God to be changeless, but I doubted it. From the beginning there has been nothing but constant change on earth—challenging and crazy-making and dazzling. Had Godde not potentiated all of it and kept abreast of every jot and tittle?

Mom's stock response to "such things" was "Boys will be boys." She looked askance at consciousness-raising efforts. In *her* book, girls were to be aloof to true intimacy, but experts at allurement with promise. I swallowed her point of view—but not whole. From Mom I got my feminism, though she would never have called it that. She worked hard to make sure the fledgling weekday nursery school at our Presbyterian church in NYC would thrive because she knew I loved books. She also knew it would help mothers and get me out of her cross hairs every morning. I have a photo of the students and the teacher I remember. I think I'm in the photo, because, though my head is bent down, you can see the bow in my black hair. Mom could organize, cheerlead, and work hard for causes. She always encouraged me to try new things, and if I failed she was still there with more encouragement—until I thought I'd choke on cheer. Still, I think that's the way I found my own way.

From Anita Hill, Madeleine L'Engle, Bishop Barbara Harris, the Rev. Lee McGee, and later, Hillary Rodham Clinton, I learned the way through: don't put them down, raise yourself up. (Mom would be on my list, but she flunked the "don't put them down" part.) I also learned this strategy from reversals Godde accomplished on behalf of so many women in Scripture.

CHAPTER 17 Mom

The night Mom lay dying, I was racing down to Connecticut to make it to her bedside, for one more . . . something. Through the salty blear of my tears, I suddenly got a clear sense of my mother's presence and remembered how hard she tried to make things work well for me, Dad, my sisters, and everyone in her life whom she loved, and some she didn't love, but adopted and tried to change. Sometimes her efforts were too much, but she tried. No one loves perfectly. Most of us try—and trying is divine.

I was speeding in mind and car. How many different ways has God tried and continues to try to connect with humanity? Some people think that the Christian idea of incarnation was the divine last-ditch effort to get our attention. I came from Mom's flesh and blood. She taught me the spirituality of trying, and honestly I think God is still trying.

Mom hadn't been dead long when I rushed in. Her mouth was stiff, agape. I could see a thin red line of bright lipstick unevenly smeared across her lips. Still prettying herself for her "man." She'd been sent to the hospital with a stomach bleed of uncertain origin, and she refused treatment—courageously lobbying for her own desires against pressure from medical staff. When she'd come "home" to die, she'd ordered a peanut butter sandwich. The nurse said, "Peggy, do you think that's a good idea?" to which my mother replied, "Can you think of a better one, darling?"

Bev had gone over to the nursing home after work and found her grandmother lying in bed, tired and alert, but not talkative. Mom pointed to the corner of the room and said, "Look at that. Don't you see? It's like an angel, a person in a white gown." Bev saw nothing and suggested she sleep while Bev held her hand.

"It was peaceful," Bev said as we hugged. "Are you okay, Mom?"

"Yeah. I'm sad," I said. "You can go on home now, sweetie, and thanks for being there with Gahmie when she died."

"Okay, I love you," she said, then left.

When I bent over Mom's lifeless body I remembered a time twenty years earlier when I'd bent over her bed after surgery. She was still under the effects of anesthesia, and I'd felt a surge of love toward her. I felt the same wash of love now. I tried to close her mouth. It seemed the dignified thing to do. Her mouth didn't budge, so I just kissed her forehead and whispered, "Goodbye, Mom. Sorry I hurt you. I love you. Goodbye."

Silently I prayed, oh God, if you do this sort of thing somewhere in the universe of all our projected heavens, tell my mother our whole story and wipe away her tears. Oh, and tell her I am happy.

I stood, looking down at Mom's frail body on the bed, dead. I'm orphaned now. Maybe God *is* like a parent, I thought, wincing at how quickly I betrayed my own mature theological distaste for such dependency metaphors. But I felt like a child. My mother had once told me that the highest calling for a woman was motherhood. I stood for what seemed a long time with my dead mother. Let's have a conversation, Mom, I heard myself murmur. She consented.

I didn't bring any wine, but . . . can we talk?

Silence.

Then: I have plenty, she said.

I said okay and went on, at the same time noticing how silly this was. But I knew people did such things and maybe Mom wasn't that far away yet. So I said, Who was your angel?

Daddy, she said.

Daddy? He sure has changed then.

No, dummy, *my* daddy. *My* daddy.

Oh, wonderful. Is Jesus there? I asked.

I don't know, she answered quickly.

You don't know?

No, darling, what does he look like?

I didn't know either. Damn! So I said, how is God? What is God like?

None of your business, dear.

Okay Mom, what I really want to know, and you know I try to know everything, to understand everything if I can. All those times when you praised me over the top and said 'I love you' too much, did you really mean it?

About half the time, darling, she said.

Tears began to flow, warm honest tears of truth. Through them I burbled, same for me, Mom. Half the time.

As I left I kissed her hand, now turning cold. I blew warm breath onto it and placed it back onto the blanket and turned away—forever, save memory echoes.

Driving home I thought to myself that our little postmortem imagined conversation proved nothing—except one thing: I knew my mother and she knew me. Such knowing counts as much as a lot of love words. It occurred to me that God and Jesus in the Bible don't go about *saying* "I love you" all the time. You just knew it. Mom and I just knew it I guess, even half-way and even through our differences. I wondered if this was what a "call" is like: you just know what you love and you do it imperfectly, and it brings you alive.

Some clergy act as if their calling was higher and more holy than any other. It's the church's fault for setting up orders of ministry and calling one order Holy Orders, and the other, what? Everyone else in the peanut gallery of pews? Doesn't work for me. What do you think, Mom? Was motherhood a holy calling for you? I swear I could hear her say "Yes, darling girl. Was daughterhood for you?" I'd miss all those *darlings*. They functioned like periods at the end of Mom's non-debatable assertions, yet they were all terms of endearment.

"This won't take long, darling" is how I imagined Mom would've said her good-byes if she could, waving us away as she turned to enter her dying, singing her favorite song from the musical *Kiss Me Kate*: "But I'm always true to you, darlin', in my fashion. Yes, I'm always true to you, darlin', in my way."

She died beautified, ready to lay her head in God's lap, the sandwich untouched, the crusts still on the bread. (She used to cut off all our peanut butter sandwich crusts and eat them herself. I'd done the same.)

After talking with my other children and Laurie, who was on vacation, I thought of Bill—how much my mother had loved him, and how hard she had tried to hang on to him. I remembered how angry I'd been that she'd kept our wedding picture prominently displayed after our divorce. But why wouldn't she? The divorce was a loss for me—and for her.

Mom's worldview was always cheery and bright; Dad's was overcast, its veracity often suspect. Mine landed in between—mixed and at times mixed up, but true. I was sure Mom hid secrets inside the sudden bursts of hostility that escaped from behind her masks of gaiety and her love for her "darlings." Now I'd never know.

Grieving for Mom wasn't tear soaked as it was for Dad, possibly because I'd been grieving her all my life—a long bumpy way along which we both had tried. Now neither of us had to try anymore. There was an ironic freedom in our final separation. No one would ever overpraise me like she did—rather a good thing, I thought. I was left only with a melancholic appreciation and time to reflect, recollect memories, and puzzle Mom's secrets, including one surprise I'd never have imagined, but one I would pursue with the same measure of tenacity it took for my mother to keep this secret so safe.

Not long after Mom's death, Laurie and I went to visit an older cousin, Peggy, the daughter of my mother's older sister, by fifteen years. After tea and cookies and back and forth family news, I said, "I've always been curious about all the high society stuff in our family. I mean, why did we all have to be in the Social Register, of all the elitist things? Was that just the times? We weren't rich and famous."

"Oh, that was because of the Jewish thing," Peggy said.

"What!" Laurie and I said in chorus, like Tweedle Dum and Tweedle Dee.

"Didn't Aunt Peggy tell you? I was a teen, I think, when Mother told me. Mother was fussed about it. Ga told all her four children after Avon had died."

"Well, she couldn't have told our mother," I said. Laurie nodded.

"I'm positive Aunt Peggy knew," Peggy said. "Maybe she found out after puberty. She wasn't married. Mother told us Ga was blasé about it all. She gathered her children and just told them." Splat like that—all over their lives.

The family secret had been released, but stuffed back into its shell quickly. My mother, and her "fussed" sister, also a Social Register aspirant, had the rest of their lives to prove the secret had nothing to do with them.

"Why didn't she tell us?" I said later to Laurie.

"Lynnie, this was Mom," Laurie said. "She never talked about feelings or the past. Remember? But isn't it exciting?"

"For sure. What a secret! Was she ashamed?" I said.

"You're too analytical. It was just her," Laurie said. "But *her* mother told."

"We have to research this, in case it's wrong," I said.

"Not wrong," we said in chorus.

I was part Jewish. No, I am part Jewish. Like my mother, Mother Church also held "secrets." Not only did I have a new window into my mother's life and much to reflect on, but I had a new lens into Jesus, whose Jewishness hadn't made it into most pulpits. I felt proud but wasn't sure exactly why. I'd always preferred Jesus on the ground, not aloft, but now my devotion to his humanity deepened. I love to talk to Godde the way Abraham did—arguing from his own righteousness, like, "Hey God, don't wipe out a whole city if ten souls in it turn up righteous. Just a thought." God *listened*.

Fleshy, breezy prayer, I thought, must be part of Jewishness. Christians can be so prim. Some blanche at divine wrath and moodiness but it helps me feel, not good, but a little less ashamed at my own nastiness. I don't freak at Jesus' moods either—angry enough to curse a little fig tree, not to mention his Sancho Panza, Peter.

I wonder if Godde takes umbrage at all our projections: *Listen. I'm not as darn omni-righteous as you would have me be—also not so controlling. How do you know what righteousness really is anyway? Ask your women, the bad ones everyone but me tried to keep hidden. I wanted them all to have voices. How moral is that? In fact, I'm the only true atheist around here. I don't believe in me as you've created me.*

Was it possible to bind God's freedom by making God a goody-goody? Godde's grace is loving but it's also knowing truth, hardly laced with political correctness. After I read the memoirs of Etty Hillesum, Jewish Holocaust victim, and the most spiritual writer I've read, I could never resort to mystical piety to escape or hide the harsh realities of life. Life stripped bare had to come first, before mysticism. It's what she learned from the experience of being a burnt offering—a holocaust. Etty taught me something about true grown-up prayer. I'd prayed desperately that my dad wouldn't die. When he did, I didn't stop praying about everything under the sun. I bet Mom prayed the same for Dad and for her own father, but death came anyway, and Mom still wanted to put her head in God's lap—or maybe her father's.

What was he like, my Jewish grandfather? I have one picture of Avon Franklin Adams—austere, not handsome, but with a kind, welcoming face and round eyeglasses. I'd stare at the photo, looking for my mother. There was a slight resemblance. "Pop" Adams, as he was called in the Manhattan music world of the 1920s, was head of the Wolfsohn Music Bureau. An impresario, he imported musical talent to America from Europe. Mom mentioned famous people like Alma Gluck, soprano and concert singer born in 1884 to a Jewish family in Bucharest, Romania, and violinist Jascha Heifitz, also born to a Jewish family, but in Lithuania. My grandfather helped Jews. Mom knew that but distanced herself by her clear preference for show tunes. "All those concerts. Boring, darling." She meant my father's weekly performances with the Mendelsohn Glee Club in New York—black tie, command performances for Dad's family. She also meant concerts she had to attend as a child. Classical music wasn't much a part of my experience growing up, but when I took Music 101 in college I was hooked as if I'd heard it all before.

After Avon died, my teenage mom was whisked off to a boarding school, which she "hated." At thirteen Mom wrote from school: "Darling Precious Mommy, I have your hanky with your sweet pure smell on it. I take it to bed with me every night it is right here beside me now so I can kiss it." From the loathsome school three years later she wrote: "Remember always that I live for you and it is for you that I try to do right and you are all that is good and glorious to me and I love you in every part of me."

I have Mom's tiny diary full of puppy love. In 1927 she wrote: "Remet and fell in love with Don Gillespie. (kissed)." Mom had told us she knew she would marry Dad the minute she met him. For her it was love at first sight and possibly her plan of salvation and ticket to guaranteed happiness—and denial. She was tenacious in her pursuit of happiness. I was tenacious too. The problem was that Mom wanted all of us to tenaciously embrace one version of happiness—hers.

Dad was a Gillespie of Morristown, New Jersey. His family wouldn't have tolerated their son marrying a Jew, or even a part Jew. His mother was an opera singer who left her career behind for marriage and children, and his father owned a business importing oils from China used to make shellac. We received sets of slick, shiny playing cards every Christmas.

The Morristown area attracted many Social Register families from Manhattan, who built estates like the Gillespie's Tower Hill, where Dad's father grew up. The Social Register of New York City was established in 1886. To get listed one had to be sponsored and could be dropped for scandals or peccadilloes, including being employed in the theater, one of my mother's early passions. (She'd had a bit part as a gun moll in a Broadway play.) The Register was a list of blue bloods and Brahmins. I used to recoil from being listed, but now I see what a vital credential the Register was for Mom.

Dad's growing-up house was not as baronial as Tower Hill but trophy enough. The post-Depression step-down house I remember had too many bedrooms to count and a long slope of green lawn I loved to roll on. Every Sunday the whole family gathered for dinner, another command performance. Fred and Lily were the servants. I loved them, especially Fred, who appeared like magic when my grandmother, a formidable pigeon-chested woman, pumped the invisible little lump buried mysteriously under the carpet. "Yes Ma'am," he'd say. Fred never would tell me exactly how this magic happened. After dinner Ma summoned "her boys" (Dad and his three brothers) to sing at the piano. Pops sat quietly in his chair, drinking and smoking a cigar. I sat at his feet and watched his cigar ash lengthen till finally he'd chuckle, wink at me, and let it drop into the standing ashtray.

Tower Hill is now a Roman Catholic school for girls, run by the Sisters of the Filipini. Dick and I visited it once and gawked at the imported carved mahogany ceilings and fireplace mantels—each one unique and one in every room. In the ornate music room, my paternal great-grandmother summoned the family every evening for prayers.

"I came from piety," I whispered to Dick.

"You came from money," he commented. "What happened?"

I jabbed him. "Yeah, but imagine the irony of this staunch old Presbyterian-suffused homestead overrun by Roman Catholic nuns."

I don't know if my mother ever told my father about her Jewish father, but if not, their move to Darien in the '50s would have sealed her lips forever. I shivered remembering the "Aryan from Darien" and *Gentlemen's Agreement*. No wonder Mom had tried so hard to be, well, Aryan.

⚛

I pursued the secret genealogy to satisfy my curiosity and, though it might seem strange, to love and honor my mother. By deductive guesswork I figured Mom's parents married in Manhattan where Avon worked. Ga's parents, the Halls of Medford, Massachusetts, had not approved, according to my cousin. Yet Ga married Avon, a Jew, on January 1, 1891. Her father was in New York at the time and did not attend the wedding, though a younger sister, Kitty, was a witness. They were married in the Church of the Strangers, formerly the Mercer Street Presbyterian Church. The church name seemed a perfect fit for a young couple estranged from part of their families.

On the marriage license, legibly, were Avon's parents' names: Adolph Adams and Marie Kaleski, both from Prussia, part of the German Empire. A Jew named Adams? Research showed three Adolph Adamses in Prussia when my Adolph would have been there. With the help of two miracle workers, a mature woman archivist and my young tech-savvy cousin, I discovered that my great-great-grandparents, the parents of Adolph, were named Hagar and Isaac. Who but Jews would have such ancient biblical names? Adolph, with Marie, twenty years younger, immigrated and showed up in the 1860 census records of Lowell, Massachusetts. He was buried in a Jewish cemetery there in 1886. This unfolding of purposefully hidden family history made me feel sad. The secret had meaning for my personal and religious identity and there was no Mom to fill in the details.

I called my favorite rabbi, a man I admired and who felt grandfatherly to me although he wasn't that much older than me. "I might be Jewish," I blurted.

"Mazeltov," he said.

"I have proof about my grandfather, but don't I need to have matrilineal proof to be sure?" I asked.

"Matrilineality has been the standard until the late twentieth century, when Reform Judaism added patrilineal descent under specific conditions, being raised in the Jewish faith with ceremony, education, and life cycle events. There is increasing conversation among Conservative rabbis about matrilineal practice but . . ." He must have felt my heart sink over the phone wires so he stopped, then added, "The biblical record, of course, is clear that patrilineality was then the rule."

"No kidding," I said. "All those fathers begetting all those sons—nary a mother or a daughter."

"There *are* women named in Matthew's genealogy. All of them women of questionable repute." We laughed.

I loved this man. Despite his rabbinical clarity, I raced to my Bible and checked. Sure enough: five women of dubious character.

Tamar seduced her father-in-law in order to have a child in the family line, which was expected by law.

Rahab, a prostitute, spied on the land and helped the ancient Israelites conquer Canaan. Bathsheba, seducee of King David the adulterer/murderer, gave birth to Solomon, second king of Israel.

Ruth, Moabitess and spurned barren widow, converted to Judaism in order to protect her equally vulnerable mother-in-law Naomi, then crafted an alliance with the landowner Boaz and went down in history as the great-grandmother of David, the royal line to Jesus.

And Mary, unwed and pregnant, took Joseph's house and lineage and soared to the top of Christian family history—as a pregnant virgin/unwed mother no less.

How did these ill-reputed women get listed in the "Social Register" of their day, the Holy Bible? Maybe the Bible wasn't the arbiter of morality it was touted to be? Maybe God wasn't as concerned with morality as with spirituality? Maybe the more outside traditional behavioral expectations you are, the closer in Godde draws you? These were not brand new wonderments for me, but I gained respect for the Holy Spirit, She to me, and Her skill as a masseuse divinely trained to smooth out all the fisted muscles in the patriarchal system. I had been massaged into the system despite moral failings.

Women were hidden like leaven in the "bread" of biblical narrative—easy to miss, just like today. The men carried the power and the numbers, but the women gave the family line vivacity. My grandmother broke rules to marry her beloved; my mother kept a secret to marry hers; and I had risked my vocation, the ire of bishops, and my children's stability to marry mine. The gumption to pursue one's heart's desires hadn't started with me; nor was I alone in feeling the emotional cost of such liberation.

My genealogy left me wonderstruck and with a softened heart for Mom. I wanted to integrate my discoveries into being a priest. A Jewish friend gave me an unexpected blessing. Over sandwiches at lunch she prayed the motzi, the traditional blessing over the bread: *Baruch atah Adonai, eloheinu melech ha-olam ha motzi lechem min ha-aretz.*

I said the blessing over and over and was intoning it as I came into the kitchen where Dick was brewing his own spaghetti sauce.

"What?" he said.

"It's the motzi. Isn't it beautiful? I learned it from a Jewish friend. Can we use it?"

"I as usual don't know what the hell you're talking about."

"Sorry. It's the blessing over the bread. Jews use it like a table grace at home and at the Shabbat meal. It means, 'Blessed are you, Lord God, King of the universe who brings forth bread from the earth.' So wouldn't it be great to start using it at St. John's for the Eucharist blessing over the bread? Authenticity. Think Jesus."

"Jesus," he said. He wiped his hands on his apron, then turned and extended the wooden spoon. "Taste this. Too salty?"

"Perfect. You did a *ha-motzi*. It means 'who brings forth.' I figure if God can bring forth bread from the earth, then God can *bring forth* lots of stuff, even grace from a wafer. You brought forth succulent sauce from a big fat tomato. Like Eucharist, no? So can we use this ancient blessing maybe?"

"It would add spice for sure. I suppose this is the new-you-Jew? What about the cup blessing?"

"I'll find out from the rabbi. I can write it up and announce it just so people won't freak out," I said.

"Since when did education prevent that? But I like it. I'll talk with the vestry and we'll see," he said and turned back to his stirring.

"It's okay to use 'sovereign' rather than 'King.' I checked." I gave Dick a hug.

That's more or less how we started using the Jewish motzi on Sundays. I used it whenever I supplied at another parish. A woman in one parish thanked me after the Eucharist: "My mother was Jewish. It brought tears." I wished my own mother could hear.

Thank God I was married to a rector. I felt happy, warm, safe—and restless inside. The twined processes of becoming a woman and a priest felt more synchronized than ever. Good. I was a woman in body and soul and a worker priest as I'd envisioned. I had a rounded religious identity. Was there more?

I went for a walk and talked.

Oh my dear Godde, please don't let me go off the rails, nuts on some obscure track. I'm ready to be steady, follow the rules, do the Gospel like I'm supposed to, stop badgering the lumbering old sow of a church about language. Do whatever you have to—but let me know first.

That night as I drifted into sleep I had a mental conversation with a wise child, young teen, my favorite age, who asked, "Is God a boy?"

"No," I answered quickly. "No, God is not a boy, and God is not a boy's name, never has been."

My inquisitor kept on. "Are you sure? What about Jesus? Some boys are named that."

Suddenly I felt like a liar. All those masculine pronouns. Who was I kidding, myself? Who was the church kidding? Tired as I was, I went on: "Well, Jesus was a man but after he died and God raised him from the dead to be with God, they called him Christ, and Christ is not a boy's name either."

"That would be so funny to meet a boy named God or Christ." The child giggled. "Or a girl."

"Well, funny things happen sometimes in the church, some funnier than others."

"Yeah, like you being Jewish like Jesus."

"Quirky, huh?" I said, and we fell asleep together.

CHAPTER 18 Keeping Madeleine's Commandment

T he century was turning over. It was time to dare and dial.

"Bishop Porteus, this is Lyn Brakeman. I wonder if we could meet and talk a bit."

"Lyn Brakeman?"

Oh God, he didn't remember me.

"You were bishop in Connecticut when I was going through the ordination process—years ago."

"Yes."

He still wasn't getting it.

"Well, you turned down my application for postulancy and I . . . I . . . well, I guess . . . I'm not angry now. But I just wanted to talk briefly."

"Oh, sure, Lyn. How about we meet at the fall convention during the break? We can have lunch together."

Lunch seemed too intimate, but I was in too far now. Massachusetts conventions were turning out to be more than church business meetings for me. At the lunch break I sought him out. He was not on the portico where we'd agreed to meet. Had he forgotten? Then I saw him propped against one of the pillars, chatting. He hadn't changed much, still twitching and jovial. I would have to go through the awkwardness of introducing myself. Summoning boldness, I approached.

"Oh hi, Lyn, How about we walk up to the Parker House?" he said.

"Okay," I said, having no idea where the Parker House was.

We walked two blocks, exchanged weather reports, and arrived at an elegant restaurant, its tables laden with heavy silverware and white table-cloths (not to the floor). We ordered our meals, twin salads. The restaurant service was very slow. The bishop fumed and looked at his watch. I hoped he noticed my collar. The lunch arrived in the middle of my speech. I waited to see if he'd say grace, but he speared a tomato wedge and I continued talking: a little history, a white lie about non-anger, and the truth about my fearful reaction to his reentry into my life. I told him I was there to take care of my shame, the historical shame I'd thought was resolved by geography alone. He listened without saying much.

I really wished he'd apologize. But honestly, the fact that my voice felt strong was recompense enough.

I watched him spear another tomato wedge and take it to his mouth. I watched him chew. Eating makes a person look so vulnerable. Finally he spoke.

"I am so glad you did this, Lyn. I am so glad. Thank you." He repeated this on and off over the tuna salad as I told him about being a worker priest. When the bill came, he paid it.

I returned to the convention jubilant, only to find Dick schmoozing and telling jokes when he was supposed to be praying for me.

After our lunch, whenever I saw Bishop Porteus at diocesan events I greeted him and he gave me a hug, always. A woman priest colleague told me that Morgan Porteus had said to her that his opposition to the ordination of women as priests was one of his more regrettable errors. He is in his late nineties now and when he dies I will cry.

When I told Lee McGee about my lunch with Porteus, we compared salient memories about the ordination struggle. Hers was not the bomb scare and all the terror she felt, but the experience of radical community in the institutional church. In small groups the whole behemoth of a church came alive. "The diocese of Washington never split as it struggled not to duck the tensions," Lee said. "They engaged in open debate in every home and parish. The diocese grew together. And we women developed such depth of personal, spiritual, and intellectual support in community."

Mine, or one of them, was also not focused on my anger, fear, or shame, but on the three male bishops who got on board for me, without a hint of condescension or overlording: Bishop Bradford Hastings, who saw Christ in Dick's and my extramarital relationship, Bishop Arthur Walmsley, who saw a priest in me and ordained her, and Bishop Morgan Porteus, who rejected me twice and after years listened to me, and paid for my lunch.

I blossomed as a priest and a woman during the Gloucester years. Dick, a feminist himself, and the spirit of the women in my family helped me keep Madeleine's commandment.

My being a religious professional working on the city's Coalition for the Prevention of Domestic Abuse was important: religion itself was like a battered woman needing a voice. Violence is a spiritual issue. Souls get as battered as bodies do, even those of perpetrators, most of them men. With local government support the Coalition wrote a proclamation and declared Gloucester a Domestic Violence Free Zone. We posted signs to proclaim the vision, very far from the lived truth, but most great visions are.

Abuse wasn't in my mother's vocabulary any more than alcoholism was, so she wouldn't have understood my domestic violence work. I imagined her voice: "So now you're going to work in the slums somewhere, darling?" But my mother would have understood Madeleine's commandment. And she would have been delighted that I landed a role in the local production of Eve Ensler's play, *The Vagina Monologues*, a way to further Ensler's goal to end violence against women and raise funds for the Coalition's work. Mom would have imagined her daughter on Broadway. She'd have overlooked the vaginas.

Of course, not everyone thinks of the *Monologues* as education or art, but most agree it is politics with a punch and a large dose of truth. My monologue was the story of a mid-life woman who went to a vagina workshop—in secret trepidation, and in hope. In the workshop, the woman discovered and explored her own wowser secrets while lying on her mat among a group of other like-matted women, all being instructed by a slim young chippy who probably had at least three vaginas, or clitorae. I wore my clerical collar in the play, was identified in the playbill as an Episcopal priest, and ad-libbed a line implying that the institutional church needed to discover her own vaginal power—and not dry up.

Six women eight-o'clockers sat in the front row. Neither Dick nor I ever heard a word from them, but I saw a grin or two. Two young women started to attend St. John's, sheepishly admitting that they came because they'd seen me in the *Monologues*. A lesbian friend in my yoga class brought her ninety-year-old mother to see the play. After seeing it she said to her daughter: "Can we go to that church?" This was V-evangelism.

More and more I understood why Madeleine had enjoined me not to become a little man. It was easy for women, even men, to get stuck in patriarchal ways or be unconscious of them. Numbers of women were in leadership roles in the church now, but women weren't immune to the seductions of clerical power and its vestiture. According to the Rev. Elizabeth Kaeton, former president of the Episcopal Women's Caucus, "Numbers are about change, but not about transformation. Transformation comes not from changing the faces at the top but from systemic change: changing hearts, changing minds, changing attitudes. We do have some women in the corridors of power who are really women dressed up in male agenda and carrying male agenda. And they aren't sisters in spirit or mission at all."

I wondered if my language agenda qualified me as a sister in mission for systemic change. My earliest spiritual experience was one of unconditional love—knowing no gender or limit. Did not attaching a gender pronoun to God set conditions on the unconditional nature of divine love? Like the Domestic Violence Free Zone signs and plays starring talking vaginas, altering theological language to liberate the patriarchal power-God was a token, but tokens eventually add up. What would happen if we women made it clear to ourselves and to the church at large that we were *not* little men, and God was *not* a big man?

Dick and I partnered for change. I joked that we had most of the Bible rewritten in our computer. It was boring work and often awkward. How many un-pronouned "Gods" can you use in one sentence? Divine titles like Master, King, Lord, and Father, were a challenge—and feminine equivalents were hilarious: Mistress, Queen, Mother, and Lady? Think ladies of the night and a hostile modifier attached to mother, which made her an f-bomb.

A friend protested to me over lunch: "On no. I don't want Jesus in a dress."

"Neither do I. But how does 'by Christ and with Christ and in Christ' sound? Or, Creator, Christ, and Holy Spirit, for Godde's multiple personality spirituality?"

"Okay, pretty good," she agreed. "But how about Her Holiness for the Spirit?"

The whole endeavor was both wonderful and, we knew, ephemeral. It would all snap back under a new rector when we left. But for now our efforts reinforced both my sense that I was trying to rescue the divine image, and that I couldn't have done it alone. "Two are better than one because they have a good reward for their toil." So wrote the wise Old Testament priest Qohelet in Ecclesiastes (4:9). When together we made language changes that were innovative and hard, our reward was in the co-creative doing.

Some appreciated it; some probably didn't notice; and some hated it. Still, we planted seeds, the fruits of which we will never know.

After fighting to get ordained in a patriarchal church, it took twenty years for me to feel secure as a woman and priest, then keep on lobbying to make sure people knew that God really wasn't a boy's name—and that girls didn't have to do mental somersaults to remind themselves that they are half the divine image. I'm impatiently aging and I don't have another twenty years in me.

A stunning piece of chronological trivia soothed my impatience: it took the biblical memoirists twenty-some years to get Jesus into gospel form.

What's another twenty, or more, to get *his* human pronoun detached from divinity?

CHAPTER 19 What's Wrong with That?

The best Christmas gift I ever received was hand delivered, took sixty-one years to arrive, was something I'd received as a child, and came from my husband Dick.

We had talked about this gift—like this:

Dick: "I saw an ad for the Rockettes. It's their seventy-fifth anniversary."

Lyn: "Oh."

Dick: "We could think about going."

Lyn: "Where?"

Dick: "To New York over Christmas to see the Rockettes and the great Christmas show."

Lyn: "You know the show?"

Dick: "Every kid who grew up in New York knows that show."

Lyn: "Every kid of means."

Dick: "Cut the sermon."

Lyn: "We can't go. New York will be a zoo over Christmas. Too expensive."

Dick ordered the tickets while I forgot about it. When they arrived, he tossed them onto the kitchen counter. I opened the envelope, annoyed at the racing of my heart. December 27, 2007. Would that be the exact same day? When I told a friend who knew my story, she squealed. "He's taking you to see the Rockettes? Wow! My husband organizes cruises, not healing events."

A healing event? I wasn't sure. I'd heard about re-traumatization. On the other hand my old god-man story had already had multiple endings and we could see the Rockefeller Center skaters, visit my first school, my apartment building, the playground—pile up good memories for ballast.

To prepare I clicked Google-god. Who were these Rockette ladies with legs like scissors—these wonders I'd longed to see and missed? The

Rockettes were the brainchild of Broadway dance director Russell Markert, himself a trained dancer and choreographer. Inspired by the Ziegfeld Follies, in 1922 Markert worked with sixteen precision dancers and by 1932, just six years before I was born, the Rockettes opened at Radio City Music Hall. I felt as awed as I had as a child. I wanted to see these dancers again. I wanted to visit my homeland in that particular way that only the past can make meaningful.

I read on: 2 3/4-inch heels, sweat-breaking auditions, kicks six inches over the head, minimum height five five. (I'm too short.) Three hundred kicks a show. I did the math: 1,200 kicks a day in a four-a-day show schedule. I was hooked. And the show started at 6 p.m., so we'd have a whole day in my city.

New York was Mom's hometown too. "New York, New York it's a wonderful town; The Bronx is up and the Battery down." She used to dance around the apartment singing this. New York was a "helluva town," we agreed. Every Christmas Mom used to take us to see department store windows alive with animated displays. We'd hear music, sacred and secular, piped all along Fifth Avenue; church bells chimed the quarter hour; outdoor Santas rang their bells for the poor and the destitute and the drunk who, not far away, slumped against buildings with their begging cups. "Can I just have a nickel, Mommy?" Clink!

"Okay let's go," I said to Dick. "Maybe it will snow."

"We'll drive to Stamford and train in from there," he said.

To me as a child Grand Central Station's domed ceiling twinkled with starry constellations and looked like a close-up of heaven. It still looked that way. I craned my neck to stare upward as rushing pedestrians bumped into me. This wasn't the first time I'd been back. It just felt like the first time.

1435 Lexington Avenue was our first stop. The green awning was still there, but no dear doorman for me to snub. In my mind was a map. "Let's walk to school," I said as I took Dick's arm in mine. "Dad used to walk us to school and every single day, almost, Laurie would drop her whole box of trading cards at the median of Park Avenue and we'd have to wait for the next light. Dad fumed."

"I can see it," Dick laughed.

As we approached Nightingale Bamford School, I pointed across the street to the apartment where Cynthia Rathbone used to live. "She had a fur coat, as the daughter of actor Basil Rathbone would. I got to try it on—not my style."

Dick, a theater buff, was impressed. "You knew Basil Rathbone?"

"No. I just slept in his bed."

I had so loved this school I'd attended through sixth grade and where I'd learned to read, write, speak some French, sing, and love learning. Except for the blue serge gunny sack uniforms, it was perfect. The students were on Christmas vacation but we got a tour. I imagined the echo of small girl voices ringing through the corridors and envisioned myself and my best friend Margy playing jacks at recess. When I later looked her up, I discovered that her father had been an Episcopal deacon, a fact I didn't know. It hadn't mattered, but suddenly it meant a lot. Had we ever talked about religion? I found Margy, but she died of cancer before we had a chance to meet. My other best friend, Carolyn, was, as I recall, Jewish. How *do* connections happen?

At lunch Dick and I sat squished into a restaurant table for two between two other tables. To our right a twenty-something daughter listened politely to her father's long speech after which she said, "Dad, I asked the question I knew you wanted to answer." She then gave her own speech, ending with, "So that's who I am, not what you wanted, but will you give me and Donna a wedding anyway?" "Okay," he said. "But can we call it a party, not a wedding?"

Dick doesn't eavesdrop as well as I do, so I filled him in. What would *our* fathers have thought? In 2003 the Episcopal Church had consecrated its first openly gay and partnered bishop, the Rt. Rev. Gene Robinson of New Hampshire. "It won't be long before there are many more," Dick said. We drank a toast to our church. (In 2008 the Episcopal Church elected and installed the bishop of Nevada the Rt. Rev. Katharine Jefferts Schori as the first woman Presiding Bishop, the church's highest office—more pastoral/symbolic than legislative/political; and by 2010 we elected and consecrated in Los Angeles the Rev. Mary Glasspool, first openly lesbian and partnered —meaning they're having sex—bishop.) Many firsts eventually make a whole tradition.

"We're besting the Presbyterians," I grinned at Dick.

The Brick Presbyterian Church on Park Avenue was next on my map. It was locked up, city style, but a woman answered the doorbell. "I'm Lyn Brakeman. I grew up in this church before my family moved to Connecticut," I said, half expecting her to recognize me.

"Oh, memory lane," she said. "I'm on duty. Oh, so what, a quick tour."

I remembered the sanctuary—ornate like an Episcopal church. The children's chapel was sweet, formal, and filled with Jesus-and-the-children images. I still have many little award pins I got for memory work. They sit now under my home altar in a teacup that was my grandmother's. After our guide left, I climbed up into the skyscraper pulpit and delivered a homily: "In the beginning there was musty fragrance. Can you sniff it here, beloved? It's the Ancient of Days, old man God, about to be stripped of all His almighty pronouns thanks to an uppity Episcopal priest who happens to be a she. Amen. Please bow your heads for the interminable pastoral prayer." Dick applauded.

"Come on, we have to head downtown," he said.

"But what about the skaters?"

"Another trip," he said, and pulled me along.

The theater line stretched around the block. As we entered I saw a large cardboard cutout of a Rockette. I stopped and stared, jostled by little girls. We took our seats in Row P on the aisle. I made sure Dick sat on my left. The lights dimmed. The din of excited children's voices died down.

The Rockettes performed as advertised—no leg astray, no beat missed. They came on, and off, then on again, in different costumes, just as Google had prophesied. "Aren't they great?" I whispered. Dick put his hand on my left leg, the one that carried my body memory of shame. I rested my hand on top of his. Together we warmed the old wound.

Visiting the scene of the crime didn't hurt me. The Rockettes were perfect, and the old "god-man" priest to my left had a mustache, no beard.

Some people ask if I've forgiven the old man in the theater. To some I say yes because I'm a Christian priest and wear some projections; to others I say no. The truth is yes *and* no. Forgiveness in Christian circles can be overdone, and too quickly an exercise in denial or steely willfulness. Still, I know forgiveness is healing and the church advances it as gospel. So I try. The old man God look-alike had nearly cost me God, but on the other hand he had set me on a quest to retrieve what I'd lost and gave me a passion to get rid of exclusively masculinizing language about Godde so no other girl or woman could possibly confuse God with a pervert as I had, or think God might be a boy's, or a man's, name.

The old man left me with scabs I don't pick. For example, it takes me time to get aroused and trust sexual surrender. My fear of the old man and my involuntary response sent my libido into partial dormancy. If I'd totally forgiven him, would I be able to do Hollywood-style sex? Hell no, and I wouldn't want it either. I learned about trauma and knew that the old man was probably acting under the tyranny of his own wounds. I've devoted countless hours to helping other women and men heal from abuse much more traumatic than mine (though no wound should be minimized by comparisons). I have my feelings, my orgasms, my body, and my God back. It took time to realize completely, that is, in my mind, my heart, *and* my body, that the old god-man in the theater *looked* like the God in my book but didn't behave at all like Godde under the table. Image isn't presence, and it is the image I am forgiving. Writing this book helped. Possibly forgiveness is a forever process, right in line with the potentiation we call creation—unfolding forever.

A year after I saw the Rockettes, another layer peeled away from the proverbial onion of emotional truth as I elevated the bread of the Eucharist and said Jesus' remembered words, "This is my body." Behind and beyond these words I heard a familiar murmur, "This is *your* body." At once I knew that what had happened to me happened to God.

余

It was February, cold to the bone. I arrived at Mercy Center feeling like a seventeen-year-old cranky teenager guarding against tears. I glanced into the chapel to see if the ugly old brass tabernacle was still there. It stood on the high altar, two feet tall, and squat with a small locked door on its belly. Inside were consecrated wafers to signal the presence of Christ—locked up, safe and sound. Why would anyone lock up Jesus, for Christ's sake?

In this chapel there used to be an arrangement of living flowers beside a china dish of consecrated wafers, open, inviting, and nested within silky pastel drapes, but it had to be dismantled by Vatican order because the Sisters of Mercy were taking too many liberties. The old tabernacle returned. To me it meant the stifling of beauty, openness, a woman's touch, and Christ's availability to all.

"Why is that ugly old tabernacle still there?" I asked my spiritual director for the week.

"You know the rules," she said. "I regret it too."

"Well, I hate it. It ruins my prayer space."

"Perhaps the tabernacle has something to say to you. Why don't you pray in front of it," she suggested.

"For the whole week?"

"You don't have to do it at all if you don't want to." She smiled.

I hate freedom.

All I wanted was to have things with God and me undisturbed—forever.

I trudged into the chapel on the first day and sat like a good girl before the self-important tabernacle. My mind wandered to a book I was reading about the Jewish Sabbath, *Sabbath World* by Judith Shulevich. You're supposed to keep *melachah*: forego your own powers and respect what is given. This tabernacle was a given. The book also said that on the Sabbath everyone is granted a *neshema yeterah*—an oversoul, like a big fleecy blanket. Well, if I make it through all seven days of this retreat I'll deserve an oversoul.

I trained my eyes from the tabernacle to the embracing beauty of the ceiling-to-floor oil painting of my sacred heart rose. Its thorns caught my attention. They could be footholds to climb up and into the giant rose, a beanstalk to heaven. The tabernacle blocked my full view. I honestly wanted to knock it down. I left the chapel.

In my room that evening I fingered the soft red petals of some Valentine roses Dick had given me. I wanted to know the rose's innards so I gently dissected one. It had fifty-three petals, velvety, delicate, white-tipped at the place where each attached to the pulpy central bud made up of thousands of thin hairs bunched together. My rose had a clean, clear scent. Its thorns could be the wounds of life, sharp at the tip and pointed downward, ready to catch an intruder. It didn't give love without a wound.

I left the petals scattered on the table and went to the window to watch the pink-topped clouds steal a last kiss of sun before they departed into the darkening night, like a parent kissing a sleeping, forgetful, earnest child.

There was evening and there was morning, the first day.

I spent part of every day that week with the tabernacle, stark against the majesty of the rose. I tried but couldn't see one without the other.

I scribbled a poem, maybe a prayer.

> Formidable
> dull, brass immensity,
> immeasurably plain
> intrusion—
> house where the blessed flesh
> and sacred blood are locked secure
> against the hungry of soul.

You stand on the threshold of a hitch in time,
the present immense.
You don't know you are about to
change from an icy monstrosity,
to a pulsing throbbing flesh and blood sacred heart—
somehow.

By day four my gaze narrowed to the lock in the door. I was locked out. Why? *"What's wrong with you?"* Were these words from the tabernacle? I repeated them. I said them kneeling, prostrate, standing, cruciform. I stood close, then far. I turned my back, then faced front. I whispered the words, then shouted them.

And there was evening and there was morning, the fourth day.

On day five I realized I'd run into the echo of my mother's words to my silent father: "What's wrong with that child?" The double wound I'd once felt with such pain whooshed back into my consciousness as I knelt before the tabernacle. I'd made these words my own and vowed to spend my life proving nothing was wrong with me.

And there was evening and there was morning, the fifth day.

The next day I rose early to see the sun's orange glow peek out from the horizon's lip. It looked to be slowly, slowly emerging yet quite quickly it popped into full glory. I'd finished a depressing review of all the locked hearts in my life, most of them, including mine, locked against the grief and fear of feeling locked out. I felt ready to dismiss forever the hurtful old words and resolved to avoid the tabernacle today.

I went instead to the greenhouse, where I saw a crown of thorns plant. The Bible story tells us that Jesus' torturers put a crown of thorns on his head, but I had no idea there was a real plant called that. Its bright orange blossoms begged me to touch them, smell them. As I bent toward the plant I saw its thorns, many tiny points covering every branch all round—much more than any rose had. I touched a flower, then a thorn, then both together.

I'd come on this retreat in the wake of a phone call from a pulmonologist informing me that my tests showed I had emphysema. Something *was* wrong with me. My mother had emphysema, another secret we found out from her doctor after she died. She didn't die from it, though it slowed her down. Comfortable by now with changing language, I wrote my own words to a familiar hymn, "Breathe On Me Breath of God." (Changing "on" to "in" was personal to my needs and also felt quite right according to Christian theology. Is God not indwelling in our flesh?)

> Breathe in me breath of God
> Healing my lungs' disease
> So that I may in purest love
> Breathe in and breathe out with thee.

> Breathe in me breath of God
> For when my life is done
> And my sweet lungs lose all their power
> My last breath and yours are one.

"What is the tabernacle teaching you?" my spiritual director finally asked.

"Nothing." She dropped the subject.

When evening passed into night I went back to the chapel—still, dark, quiet, the day erased. I stared at the tabernacle and prayed, "You locked me out so I locked you out. It was too big an ache, Mommy, too much to bear, too much bursting heart."

Instead of an answer, I heard myself say out loud, "What's wrong with that?" Eerily calm, I knelt and recited a litany, a scourge, every possible thing that was wrong with me, a cross so false, so full of circular suffering, so full of myself it would have put even Godde to sleep, were it not for its refrain: *What's wrong with that?*

I'm too ambitious. *What's wrong with that?* My mother locked me out. *What's wrong with that?* The church is full of shit. *What's wrong with that?* I consecrate the putative body and blood and think I'm a priest. *What's wrong with that?* Your skirts are too short. *What's wrong with that?* I got ordained to prove there was nothing wrong with me. *What's wrong with that?* I think I made God up—myself too. *What's wrong with that?* I've been selfish. *What's wrong with that?* I have emphysema now and I hate my mother, but my mother gave me God. *What's wrong with that?* Godde is NOT a man! *What's wrong with that?* I want to be a thornless rose, not a tabernacle. *What's wrong with that?* I locked my heart. *What's wrong with that?*

To every accusation my mind conjured, I flung back the refrain. Was I expecting the tabernacle to answer, or was I answering for the tabernacle or God or Jesus or what? I felt slightly insane. What was wrong with that? My feet tingled and let me know it was time to move. I rubbed them into life. They took me to bed. God had left me jagged, uncertain. Suddenly I thought of my mother, feeling locked out of her mother's heart.

A full moon splashed its light all over my room, shining through the shadeless windows, falling over the table laden with my unread books and rose petals, traveling across the chair where I'd sat, and crawling up onto the edge of my bed. I slept with the moon.

And there was evening and there was morning, a sixth day.

This retreat, an exorcism of sorts, left me drained and famished. If they have pancakes for breakfast, I'll have two helpings instead of my usual cereal, I asserted. What could be wrong with that? Nothing wrong with one more chapel visit either. I stood before the tabernacle. It looked neither friendly nor hostile.

Open it, I told myself; you're a priest, you know where the key's kept. In the sacristy I opened many small drawers before I found it—a tiny key, dangling from a red ribbon at the back of the fourth drawer from the left. I carried it back and approached the altar and the tabernacle. I inserted the key in the lock, a perfect fit, but I didn't turn it yet. When I did, I didn't pull the door open right away. I knew what was in there, so why did my heart thrum? It told me it was strong enough to support my weakened lungs. It told me I was potentiated. I pulled the door open.

Inside there was a tiny world on a round white stage, covered with white glossy fabric like satin. I slid the white curtain slowly aside with my thumb and forefinger. On stage stood a miniature ciborium that looked like a chalice with a top. There was a cross on top of it, with a white chapel veil draped over it. The cross poked through a tiny buttonhole sewn in the veil, just the right size to let it rise above the secret little scene.

Some woman set this scene with the utmost precision, as a child would set up her doll house, every figure in its place. I lifted the veil, removed the top from the ciborium, and picked up one wafer—delicate, white. I held it up to the window's light to see if it was translucent, but it was solid. I caressed it, then ate it, letting it dissolve and become part of me. Split-secondly, as in a dream, I was under the old dining room table again— me, Godde, Christ, religion, spirituality, everyone I'd ever loved, the whole hodgepodge of god-ness—all at once one.

So this is the content of a locked heart—the gift of life, exquisite, small, naked, true, holy, and painful.

What's wrong with that?

I reassembled the array with care, locked the tabernacle and gave it a pat, nodded to the rose, returned the key to its rightful place, and left.

And there was evening and there was morning, the seventh day.

Epilogue

There is always a story for the story for the story, just like memory. Here is a fascinating one.

After years of writing, revising, more writing, and researching possible publishers, I finally got a publishing offer at Easter, 2015—lovely coincidence. I was thrilled of course and signed the contract. Just getting that far seemed sufficient. I didn't care about money, big sales, and all the mechanics of launching a book—yet. I felt the same as I did when I first thought of approaching the church to be ordained priest: excitedly naive. In addition, I was getting old—and older. What would I have to do next?

As it turned out the publisher requested a lot of help with marketing. Who would know the market audience better than me? That made sense, so I became as alert and clever a marketer as I could. Then of course I reread the entire manuscript before I sent it in. Have it in very good shape, they said. This got me chuckling as I recalled stories of heroic editors who recognized and rescued greatness from unruly manuscripts that arrived in bloated or shabby condition.

I think editors are to great literature what Saint Paul the apostle was to Jesus the Christ. But I'm no saint, or great, so I spent time—lots of it—on my manuscript. Sometimes I thought, *Jeez, do I want to say this, like that?* But mostly I liked what I'd written, and it felt new. Let me tell you that it is very good practice to let a piece of work lie fallow for a year.

But I wouldn't advise leaving the acquisition of permission for direct quotes till last. Getting permissions to quote from other works I thought would be easy. The Bible, by the way, is not in the public domain. Ironic, but when I think of the many translations, and that it is still a best seller, I understand. However you can quote up to 500 lines before you need permission. The Book of Common Prayer of the Episcopal Church however is in the public domain, so quote away.

When you run into publishing goliaths, whose websites are worse than "Greek," you may, as I did, decide that your own words are sufficient to narrate for meaning without a direct quote—except for one I simply had to use from *The Little Book About God* by Lauren Ford. One scene pictured God listening for "weeny sounds"—like the ones I was making as a child. I had to quote the words that connected me to the presence of God, words I hold dear today.

I still have my original book and still hold dear its words. It was published by Doubleday in 1934, has no ISBN number, and is out of print. I found out that Doubleday/Random no longer holds the copyright for the book. The copyright reverted to the author. Thanks to Google-god, a phone call taken by a kind woman at Random House, a Benedictine sister, and a tiny historical society in North Bethlehem, Connecticut where Lauren Ford's artwork is preserved, I learned that she died in 1973—and that a book does not revert to the public domain until seventy years after an author's death. That brought me to 2043. Now what?

Who was the woman who wrote my lines? Lauren Ford was a revered local artist in Bethlehem. She lived on a farm she called Sheepfold, after the sheep who resided there and whom Ford loved. Sheepfold eventually became the birthplace of the Abbey of Regina Laudis. Ford had offered hospitality to the abbey's foundress, Mother Benedict Duss (American, Vera Duss) when she arrived from France in 1947. Near the end of World War II, living in fear of German hostility, Mother Benedict had climbed the tower of the Abbey of Jouarre in France to overlook the land. She spotted troops approaching and recognized that they were American, part of General George Patton's army. In response to this dramatic "lifting of oppression" by American troops, Mother Benedict, an American herself, felt the call to "plant monastic life in America."

Getting this permission was taking me on another great adventure, not my own, through history with religious roots.

Robert Leather, a Bethlehem industrialist, and devout Congregationalist, owned a large piece of land on a hill where he prayed. He wished the hill to be held intact in perpetuity so he gave the land to Mother Benedict and the sisters. It is the centerpiece of their abbey today. It is worth noting that, although Reverend Mother faced many obstacles along the way, she received significant support for her efforts from the Papal Nuncio to Paris—who would become Pope John XXIII, famous for initiating the liberating reforms of Vatican II.

Do you see how the Holy Spirit works to make connections we could never dream would happen? For me, it recalled my youthful wannabe Roman Catholic yearnings, my love for the God Lauren Ford's book showed me as a child, and the incredible gift of prayer which has sustained me all my life.

The Abbey of Regina Laudis is home to a community of cloistered contemplative Benedictine sisters dedicated to the praise of God through prayer and work. Their mission to praise God at all times has as its motto a phrase from the book of Judith—*Non recedat laus: Let praise never cease!* And was it not the biblical story in the book of Judith that re-enlivened me after the patriarchal church had first rejected my application for postulancy?

The abbey sisters still raise sheep at Sheepfold. It's a very strenuous job, especially midwifing a lamb's birth. They sell cheeses, jams of the fruit of the land, scarves woven of sheep's wool by community artisans, CDs of their chanting, perfumes created in their *Reine de Saba* (Queen of Sheba) herb department, and other monastic art. Guests are welcome to spend time in guest cottages at the abbey to pray and be open to the presence of God—just what I did as a child under the dining room table where God heard my "weeny sounds."

And get this for connection: Mother Dolores Hart, OSB, current prioress of the abbey, was a former Hollywood star. Remember my mother's passion for showtime and theater? Hart acted in plays and in many films, one opposite Montgomery Clift, my favorite actor when I was a teen. Swoon! She made her film debut, with Elvis Presley, in 1957 in *Loving You*. She also had a role in *Where The Boys Are* (I loved that one!) and starred in the film *Francis of Assisi* in 1961. She played Saint Clare of Assisi, foundress of the religious monastic order for poor ladies in the Franciscan tradition. The order is commonly called the Poor Clares. Hart, who had converted to Roman Catholicism at the age of ten, eventually followed a call to take on a vowed life; however, she never abandoned her love of theater. It became part of her ministry at the convent to help young people find Christ through the theatrical arts. Every summer on the abbey's 400 rural acres the thirty-eight nuns help the local community put on a musical.

Rev. Mother Dolores Hart wrote a book with Richard DeNeut, called *The Ear of The Heart: An Actress's Journey from Hollywood to Holy Vows,* published in 2013 by none other than Ignatius Press. Remember the hero of the Spiritual Exercises and founder of the Society of Jesus, Jesuits, and my own Jesuit Pierre Wolff from whom I learned to know Jesus by heart? We both ended up priests in the Episcopal Church.

There's no end to the work of the Holy Spirit making connections we could never dream would happen? *Her* latest assistant on earth is Internet technology which we access with the WWW. I take that to mean *world wide worth*.

But I still needed my permission. Pursuing one clue I got from the president of the historical society, I tracked down a great granddaughter in Bethlehem. The book was written for her grandmother, she told me, and listened as I told her what I wanted and why. She remembered the scene I had loved, even the "weeny"sounds. I felt compelled to explain my odd title but it didn't seem to bother her at all. I guess she too knows the God in her granny's book.

Surely the mission of *The Little Book About God* must have been: portray a sense of the presence of God that even a child can grasp. My book takes that child into adulthood, still inspired by the listening presence. So there is the adventure story about how I got my most significant yet *weeniest* permission.